SAT® Vocabulary

A New Approach

Larry Krieger and Erica L. Meltzer

◣ THE CRITICAL READER

New York

ISBN-13: 978-0-9975178-4-2
ISBN-10: 0997517840

Table of Contents

Introduction

A short time ago, in a galaxy not too far away, students just like you took a college admissions exam featuring "obscure" words like *vitriolic*, *sardonic*, and *vituperative*. An organization called ETS tested these words on questions called sentence completions, and teachers and tutors around the world finished each lesson by earnestly urging their students to "study your vocabulary." Then, something extraordinary occurred. The College Board decided to write the SAT® itself and promptly announced that these so-called obscure words and sentence completions would be banished from the test. Students cheered and stopped studying long lists of vocabulary words.

These celebrations, however, seem to have been premature. While the College Board did banish all of the sentence completions and traditional vocabulary words, it replaced them with a new set of words—one that was not necessarily less challenging. As we have discovered, many students are uncertain about the meaning of words such as *underpinning* and phrases such as *arrant purposelessness*. And that in turn led us to ask a question: exactly what role does vocabulary play on the new SAT?

This question prompted us to launch an exhaustive (and exhausting) analysis of vocabulary on both the new Reading Test and the new Writing and Language Test. We also took a close look at the new Essay. Our analysis revealed that vocabulary continues to play a significant role on the exam. However, that role is subtler than it was on the old SAT. Instead of being concentrated in 19 sentence completions and a handful of vocabulary-in-context questions, the new SAT vocabulary takes a variety of different forms.

Our findings convinced us that the new SAT requires a new approach to vocabulary. In the past, SAT prep books featured long lists containing hundreds of alphabetized words. This book does not do that. Instead, we have devoted a chapter to the following four specific types of vocabulary questions:

1. Vocabulary In Context
2. Passage-Based Vocabulary
3. Commonly Confused Words
4. Transitional Words and Phrases

Each chapter provides carefully sequenced sets of guided and independent practice questions, followed by detailed explanations.

We conclude this book with a special section on the new SAT Essay. Although this portion of the test is optional, a majority of students are choosing to sit for it. In addition to providing a general template for constructing a strong five-paragraph essay, we provide students with specific examples of how to use effective transitions and a strong descriptive vocabulary to achieve a high score. The chapter concludes with a student essay that earned a top score of 24 on an actual exam.

We have written this book with two main goals. First, we strive to present an enjoyable and stimulating course. And second, we strive to teach content and skills that will help all students excel on the SAT.

Good luck on your exam!

Larry Krieger and Erica L. Meltzer
February 2017

Part I: Reading

Chapter 1: Vocabulary in Context

Vocabulary-in-context questions appear on the SAT Reading Test. They are designed to gauge your ability to use contextual clues to determine the meaning of a word or phrase that has multiple definitions, or that is being used in an unusual way within a passage.

You can essentially think of these questions as a matching game. The passage will contain key words or phrases that correspond to one of the answers among the choices; your job is to connect those key elements of the passage to the correct answer.

These questions make up a significant portion of the exam—approximately 15%. You can assume that your test will include between seven and nine of them, representing a total of about 50 points on the 800-point scale. Because they appear so often, you must have a clear plan for working through them. We'll go into specific strategies later, but first let's look at what these questions involve.

The good news is that vocabulary-in-context questions are always phrased the same way:

- As used in line x, "common" most nearly means...

These questions are guided by one major principle: **context determines meaning**.

In some cases, that meaning will be reasonably close to a word's literal or most frequently used definition. In other cases, however, it may be entirely different. As a result, you should be careful not to make too many assumptions based on what a word typically means.

Let's start by considering the meaning of the word *common* in the context of the following sentence:

> She didn't see herself as a hero but simply as a **common** citizen.

Since the sentence tells us that the woman didn't see herself as a hero, we are looking for a definition of *common* that means the opposite of "hero." Within the context of this sentence, *common* means "ordinary," its usual definition.

Now, consider the meaning of the word *yield* in this short passage:

> The launch of a sustained program to develop green alternatives such as wind and solar power will **yield** numerous benefits. It will end our dangerous dependence upon importing oil from nations that are often hostile to our national interests and will spur economic growth by creating new industries and new jobs.

If you're accustomed to encountering the word *yield* in relation to driving, your first instinct might be to associate it with letting someone else go ahead of you. However, that meaning doesn't make sense in this context. Rather, the phrases *numerous benefits* and *spur economic growth* indicate that this word has a much more positive connotation here. It must mean something like "create."

6

Although vocabulary-in-context questions focus on common, everyday words, they can also be surprisingly subtle and tricky. As a result, you should not underestimate them. In some cases, the answer choices may consist of four relatively similar words, in which case you will need to distinguish very carefully among them in order to determine the correct option.

Another challenging aspect of studying for vocabulary-in-context questions is the fact that they tend to be quite random. Unfortunately, there is no set list of words from which questions are repeatedly drawn. (That said, we have included a list of words commonly used in their second meanings at the end of this chapter). The good news is that there are a number of strategies that can help you work through these questions effectively and minimize the chance that you will second-guess yourself.

Recognizing Context Clues

Although it might seem obvious, the "context" aspect of vocabulary-in-context is absolutely key to approaching these questions. More than anything, the ability to identify context clues will help you understand what type of word you are looking for and prevent you from getting sidetracked—either by meanings you normally associate with a word or by plausible-sounding distractors that don't quite fit the definition required by the passage.

So how do you know what to focus on? Let's look at some examples.

Example #1

Auto dealers in Hawaii support the transition to renewable energy, but they believe it will take a massive advertising campaign by the state to encourage people to buy vehicles powered by
5 alternative fuels. Hawaii's residents ranked second in the nation in 2015 with 2.94 electric vehicles for every 1,000 residents, just behind California, according to the U.S. Department of Energy. In contrast, tackling the fossil fuels used in airplanes will
10 have to wait. Hawaii lies nearly 2,500 miles from the continental United States, so air travel is **critical** to the state's tourism industry; however, long flights require energy in a dense form that is currently only available in fossil fuels.

1

As used in line 11, "critical" most nearly means

The first thing to notice is that this question concerns a word located at the very end of the passage. As a result, you might not be quite sure where to look for clues. After all, the passage contains a fair amount of information, so the context clues you need could be located almost anywhere, right? Well, actually, probably not.

In reality, **clues to most vocabulary-in-context questions will appear fairly close to the words themselves: if not in the same sentence, then in the sentence before or after. Those are the sentences you should plan to focus on, regardless of how long a passage is.**

In this case, what do we learn from the sentence in which the word *critical* appears? That Hawaii is nearly 2,500 miles from the continental U.S.

Given that information, we can logically conclude that air travel must play a very large role in the state's tourism industry; there aren't any other ways to cover that type of distance easily. The word *critical* must therefore mean something like "important."

Now consider the answers:

    A) insecure.
    B) weak.
    C) essential.
    D) resistant.

The only word that matches is *essential*. Logically, air travel would indeed be essential to tourism in Hawaii because the state is located so far from the mainland. C) is thus the answer.

Example #2

Though their work is invisible to the public, the imprint of copy desks on newsroom culture is enormous. Desk chiefs are still called slots, recalling the days when they functioned as slots through which
5 **raw** stories <u>were sent to be checked</u> and finished stories were dispatched to the composing room.

1

As used in line 5, "raw" most nearly means

Raw is a word that's normally associated with food, so the use of this word in the context of newsrooms might seem somewhat odd to you. However, it's precisely that context that matters most.

Again, we're going to start by focusing on the sentence in which the word appears. What does that sentence tell us about "raw" stories? That they were *sent to be checked*. So a "raw" story is a story that has not been checked.

Now consider the answers:

    A) unedited.
    B) divulged.
    C) evident.
    D) immature.

Right away, A) should pop out at you. A story that still needs to be checked (that is, proofread or verified) is an *unedited* story. In addition, this answer is clearly consistent with the idea of a newsroom. A) is thus correct.

Note that if you do this type of work upfront, it does not matter whether you know what *divulged* (revealed) means. The wording of the passage points directly to A), and so there is no need to be concerned with the other options—regardless of whether you know their definitions.

Example #3

For several years, scientists working with the Japanese Space Agency (JAXA) studied the effects of life aboard the International Space Station for a small school of medaka fish. Also known as Japanese rice
5　fish, medaka are small, freshwater fish native to Japan. They are also invaluable for space research. Not only are they easy to breed, but they are transparent, giving researchers a clear view of their bones and organs as they adjust to life in space.

1 ▰▰▰▰▰▰▰▰▰▰▰▰▰▰▰▰

As used in line 8, "clear" most nearly means

The passage indicates that researchers have a "clear" view because the fish are *transparent*. In other words, there's nothing blocking the researchers' view.

- A) keen.
- B) luminous.
- C) sheer.
- D) unobstructed.

Not blocked = *unobstructed*, so D) is correct. To reiterate: if you can make that connection, it does not matter whether you know the definitions of any of the other words.

Example #4

Recent studies suggest that ride-sharing services could do a much better job providing useful information to drivers. For example, one current app provides heat maps to show drivers where they are
5　most likely to get rides, but only when surge pricing is in effect and demand is strong. But it doesn't help drivers figure out how to optimize their business during the doldrums, when demand is poor.

1 ▰▰▰▰▰▰▰▰▰▰▰▰▰▰▰▰

As used in line 8, "poor" most nearly means

The key phrase is *during the doldrums*, which refers to a period of sluggishness or inactivity. This phrase indicates that the sentence is talking about a time when drivers do not have a lot of business.

But what do you do if you don't know what the "doldrums" are? Well, in that case you can still figure out the answer—it'll take a little more work. Notice that the beginning of the last sentence begins with *but*, indicating a contrast between that sentence and the previous sentence.

What is the focus of the previous sentence? Times when demand for rides is *strong*. Logically, then, the last sentence must be discussing the opposite situation: times when demand is **not** strong.

Now consider the answers:

- A) outdated.
- B) mournful.
- C) modest.
- D) weak.

Since *weak* is the direct opposite of *strong*, D) is the clearest fit.

9

Example #5

These days, various entrepreneurs are betting they can build radically new vehicles using a tiny fraction of the investment that was once required. These would-be carmakers are raising money through
5 online crowdfunding, taking money in small amounts from people who in many cases have only modest incomes. There's a lot of faith involved, in other words—on the part of the entrepreneurs, who are betting on their ability to beat the auto industry at its
10 own game, as well as the small investors putting up a few dollars at a time.

As used in line 9, "betting on" most nearly means

The sentence in which the phrase appears contains the key piece of information, but you must back up all the way to the beginning of the sentence to find it. Don't make the common mistake of starting after the dash.

What do we learn from the beginning of the sentence? That *there's a lot of faith involved.* So basically, *betting on* means something like "having faith." That's a very important piece of information to keep in mind when you look at the answers.

    A) pledging to.
    B) gambling with.
    C) raffling off.
    D) confident in.

The answer most closely related to the idea of having faith is D). Someone who has faith is by definition someone who has a lot of confidence.

If you hadn't established that relationship upfront, there's a decent chance you might have fallen for B), *gambling with*, because that is the definition you are most naturally inclined to associate with the idea of betting. In addition, the references to *beat[ing] the auto industry at its own game* and *investors putting up a few dollars at a time* might seem to support the idea of gambling.

However, the question does not ask whether the passage suggests that entrepreneurs are gambling with people's money. It only asks what *betting on* means right where it is placed in the sentence. When you plug both options into the sentence, only *confident in* makes sense. Logically, entrepreneurs are not gambling with their *ability*. The whole point is that they feel confident in their ability!

In addition, **it's usually safe to assume that if an answer involves the most common meaning of a word, then that answer is probably wrong.** If the word were used literally, there wouldn't be much of a reason to test it in the first place.

Further Strategies

Beyond using context clues, there are some additional strategies that can help you narrow down answers and avoid getting distracted either by trick answers or by your pre-existing knowledge.

1) Cross out the word in the passage

If you consistently get distracted by the usual meaning of the word in the passage, you may find it helpful to take your pencil and <u>quickly</u> scratch that word out in your test. Removing it from your line of vision will allow you focus on the meaning in context and override any existing associations.

2) Plug in your own word and then find the answer that matches

This is often a highly effective strategy, one that can help you rapidly zero in on the answer and prevent you from getting fooled by plausible-sounding but not-quite-right distractors.

But a **warning**: in order for this strategy to be effective, you must work quickly. If you need more than a few seconds, you'll probably end up wasting too much time and overthinking things.

The other potential stumbling block is that even if you supply an accurate synonym, the correct answer may be just different enough that you have trouble connecting your word to it. If you are generally a strong reader, however, this should not pose a serious problem.

3) Play positive/negative, then plug in

If you can determine from context whether the word is positive or negative, you can sometimes eliminate an answer or two. You can then plug the remaining answers back into the sentence and see which one makes the most sense. In rare cases, you may even be able to eliminate three options and jump directly to the answer.

This strategy is ideal for a question like Example #1 on p. 7. As we determined from the context (*Hawaii lies nearly 2,500 miles from the continental United States, so air travel is critical to the state's tourism industry*), the word *critical* must mean something like "important." That's clearly a positive word.

Now, let's just reconsider the answer choices on their own:

A) insecure. (negative)
B) weak. (negative)
C) essential. (positive)
D) resistant. (negative)

The only positive option is *essential*, which is also the answer.

4) Plug each answer choice into the sentence

If playing positive/negative is not helpful way to approach a question, or you are having difficulty plugging in your own word, plugging each word into the passage is another way to prevent yourself from getting stuck. Frequently, you will be able to hear that a particular choice does not sound correct or have the proper meaning within the context of a sentence. The only potential downside is that sometimes, as is true for #1, the right answer is not a word you would think to use. As a result, you might talk yourself out of choosing it because you think it sounds too odd.

Additional Points

While some people feel most comfortable using a single approach for all vocabulary-in-context questions, certain questions do lend themselves better to certain approaches. On some questions, inserting your own word may be sufficient to get you to the answer, while on others a combination of positive/negative and plugging in answer choices might be most effective.

Regardless of which strategy or strategies you choose to employ, remember that you should **never eliminate a word solely because you do not know what it means, or choose a word solely because you do know what it means**. Your knowledge of a word has exactly zero effect on whether it is correct or incorrect. *Zero.*

At the same time, you must avoid becoming distracted by what you don't know. Say that you're working on a question and have eliminated two answers. You're absolutely certain about the definition of one of the words, and it creates a logical meaning when you plug it in. The other word has a meaning you're not really sure about. What do you do? *You pick the first word.* If you know the meaning of a word, and it's clearly a good fit, it's the answer. The other option is simply there to distract you. It's your job not to let that happen.

So remember: always work from what you do know to what you don't know. And if a word you don't know is the only answer left after you've conclusively eliminated all of your other options, then you can pick that word with a high degree of confidence.

And to reiterate: context clues are most likely to be placed in the immediate vicinity of the word— if not in the same sentence, then in the sentence before or after. Only if you cannot find the necessary information in one of those places should you extend your range.

On the following page, we'll look at how these strategies apply in practice.

Guided Practice

Example #1

Nat Turner's rebellion came at a crucial time, more than two decades after the 1808 banning of the trans-Atlantic slave trade in **1808. By 1831, abolitionists were using the accounts** of former
5 slaves to illustrate its horrors.

As used in line 4, "accounts" most nearly means

A) debates.
B) descriptions.
C) values.
D) estimates.

The fact that abolitionists were using the "accounts" to illustrate the horrors of slavery suggests that this word refers to what former slaves said or wrote about their experiences. If you plugged in your own word, you might say something like *stories*. There is no word with that exact meaning among the choices, however, so you must select the option closest to it.

Debates, values, and *estimates* aren't the same as stories, but *descriptions* is pretty close. When you plug it back into the passage, it makes sense: logically, descriptions of slavery would *illustrate its horrors*. B) is thus correct.

Example #2

Once a common sight, the rusty patched bumblebee (*Bombus affinis*) is now hovering precariously on the brink of extinction. Over the past two decades, its population has declined by almost 90
5 percent. The rusty patched bumblebee joins seven species of Hawaiian bees that have already been declared endangered. The threats those seven species are facing resemble the ones that have depleted the rusty patched bumblebee: loss of habitat, diseases and
10 parasites, pesticides, and climate change.

As used in line 8, "facing" most nearly means

A) confronting.
B) repelling.
C) achieving.
D) directing.

Let's start by considering the context. The passage and the sentence in which the word appears are both discussing the disappearance of bumblebees. That's a negative thing. *Achieving* is positive, so right away you can eliminate C).

There's nothing in the passage to indicate that the bees are *repelling* (fighting off) the threats. On the contrary, the fact that the bees are endangered implies that they are being weakened by the threats. B) can therefore be eliminated as well.

D), *directing,* is also somewhat positive and does not make sense at all: this word implies that the bees are managing or controlling the threats, but that's clearly not the case here.

The only word that makes sense is *confronting,* which is consistent with the idea of a threat. A) is thus correct.

Example #3

As part of their study of giant sequoias, scientists have measured exactly how much water these trees require. During the summer, each tree pumps up around 2,000 liters of water from the ground, a
5 number that could climb as high as 3,000 liters a day for the largest specimens during the hottest weather. Even so, by closing their leaf pores, or stomata, and dropping some of their leaves, the sequoias are able to weather droughts with surprising resiliency

1

As used in line 5, "climb" most nearly means

A) increase.
B) escalate.
C) clamber.
D) improve.

2

As used in line 9, "weather" most nearly means

A) uphold.
B) surpass.
C) permit.
D) withstand.

Question #1: The sentence is talking about the usual 2,000 liters of water required by giant sequoias during the summer vs. the 3,000 liters required on the hottest days. 3,000 is obviously larger than 2,000, so the correct word must mean something like "rise" or "increase." If you plug in either word, you should be able to jump to A) right away. The match is so exact that you do not even need to consider the other options. Do not, for example, get distracted if you don't know what *clamber* (climb awkwardly) means. As long as you know that A) works, the definition of *clamber* is irrelevant.

Question #2: Although this question appears to be testing only the meaning of *weather*, it's actually testing two words simultaneously. If you do not have at least an approximate sense of what *resiliency* in the following sentence means, this question becomes very difficult to answer.

Let's start by summarizing that section of the passage. Basically, it's saying that even though sequoias require a huge amount of water in very hot weather, they are unexpectedly able to survive droughts. Given that, *weather* must mean something like "survive" or "get through." If you can draw a relationship between one of those definitions and *withstand*, then you can jump right to D).

Otherwise, you can work by process of elimination, plugging in each option to see whether it makes sense in context. A), *uphold* (support), does not make sense because droughts are not something that water-dependent trees would want to support. Likewise, it does not make any sense to say that sequoias are able to *surpass* (exceed, do better than) droughts. That is not the same thing as surviving, so B) can be eliminated as well. Likewise, C), *permit*, does not describe something that a tree can do to a drought—there's just no relationship. That leaves D). Even if you're not entirely sure about *withstand*, it is the only option that remains.

Example #4

Coral reefs can begin to die for a lot of reasons. Low oxygen level in the water is one example. When coral polyps are ailing, they tend to expel the symbiotic single-celled plants called zooxanthellae
5 that give corals their color and the nutrients they need to survive. The corals take on a white, bleached appearance. If they don't manage to get their zooxanthellae healthy within a few weeks, the corals usually will not survive.

1

As used in line 3, "expel" most nearly means

A) irritate.
B) drive out.
C) exhaust.
D) suspend.

This is a stellar example of a question in which context clues point straight to the answer. In this case, however, it is necessary to read both the sentence in which the word appears AND the following sentence in order get the full picture.

The initial sentence tells us that zooxanthellae, the plants being expelled, *give corals their color*, and the following sentence indicates that corals lose their color (*a white, bleached appearance*). Why would that happen? Because the plants that give the corals color are no longer present. In other words, the plants have been *driven out*. Only B) captures the correct idea; the other options do not explain why the color-giving plants would be absent.

Example #5

My godmother lived in a handsome house in the clean and ancient town of Bretton. Her husband's family had been residents there for generations, and bore, indeed, the name of their birth-place—Bretton
5 of Bretton: whether by coincidence, or because some remote ancestor had been a personage of sufficient importance to leave his name to his neighbourhood, I know not.
    When I was a girl I went to Bretton about twice a
10 year, and well I liked the visit. The house and its inmates specially suited me. The large peaceful rooms, the well-arranged furniture, the clear wide windows, the balcony outside, looking down on a fine antique street, where Sundays and holidays seemed
15 always to abide—so quiet was its atmosphere, so clean its pavement—these things pleased me well.

1

As used in line 15, "abide" most nearly means

A) obey.
B) inhabit.
C) take place.
D) tolerate.

This question is a little trickier than some of the others we've looked at so far because it contains fewer direct clues for the answer. Rather, you must determine the meaning from the general situation described. A combination of strategies is therefore most likely to be effective.

Start by figuring out what's going on in the sentence where the word *abide* appears. Essentially, the narrator is describing some positive aspects of Bretton (*peaceful rooms, well-arranged furniture, fine antique street*), so it is reasonable to assume that the correct answer will **not** be negative. *Obey, occur,* and *inhabit* are all pretty neutral, but *tolerate* has somewhat of a negative implication. People don't tolerate *things that please [them] so well*, so D) can be eliminated.

Next, plug in each word:

A): *The large peaceful rooms... where Sundays and holidays seemed always to obey.*

No, that's silly. Sundays and holidays can't "obey" anything.

B): *The large peaceful rooms... where Sundays and holidays seemed always to inhabit.*

Again, that doesn't make sense. Sundays and holidays can't "inhabit" anything. B) is out too.

C): *The large peaceful rooms... where Sundays and holidays seemed always to take place.*

That makes a reasonable amount of sense. Days and holidays can "take place." Besides, none of the other options fits at all. So by process of elimination, C) must be correct.

Independent Practice: Set #1

1.   This ability to judge the limits and capabilities of one's own memory is known as meta-memory, and a new study is shedding light on how this phenomenon works in the brain. Scientists now know that
5 primates—and possibly other animals such as rats or birds—display some form of meta-memory ability. For example, a bird may choose to not waste time searching an area for food if it is more certain that food can be found in a different area. However, so far
10 no one has been able to pinpoint what part of the brain is involved in this crucial process.

1

As used in line 3, "shedding light on" most nearly means

A) adapting.
B) disposing.
C) revealing.
D) shimmering.

2.   For the past two years, Stanford genetics professor Michael Snyder and his research team have been compiling the results from roughly 60 volunteers—himself included—who have been
5 diligently tracking their bodies' behaviors through wearable biosensors. All those devices—some people wore half a dozen—collected more than 250,000 measurements a day on everything from heart rate to blood oxygen levels to skin temperature
10 to physical activity to sleep patterns.

2

As used in line 5, "tracking" most nearly means

A) stalking.
B) chasing.
C) following.
D) monitoring.

3.   It seems obvious that a group of people with diverse individual expertise would be better than a homogeneous group at solving complex, nonroutine problems. It is less obvious that social diversity
5 should work in the same way—yet the science shows that it does. This is not only because people with different backgrounds bring a variety of information and perspectives. Simply interacting with individuals who are different forces group members to prepare
10 more deeply, to anticipate alternative viewpoints and to expect that reaching a consensus will take effort.

3

As used in line 10, "deeply" most nearly means

A) thoroughly.
B) distantly.
C) abysmally.
D) obscurely.

4.   In those days, and later as a young man, I used
to try to picture in my imagination the feelings and
ambitions of a white boy with absolutely no limit
placed upon his aspirations and activities. I used to
5   envy the white boy who had no obstacles placed in
the way of his becoming a Congressman, Governor,
Bishop, or President by reason of the accident of his
birth or race. I used to picture the way that I would act
under such circumstances; how I would begin at the
10 bottom and keep rising until I reached the highest
round of success.

4

As used in line 11, "round" most nearly means

A) aspect.
B) procession.
C) rung.
D) enclosure.

5.   For millennia humans have gazed into the night
sky and dreamed of traveling to the stars. Now that
people have walked on the moon and lived in orbit on
the space station, it seems inevitable that we will
5   venture farther, to Mars, the rest of the solar system
and beyond. The dream is common to many cultures
and occupies the space agencies of nations around the
world.

5

As used in line 6, "common to" most nearly means

A) surrounded by.
B) acceptable to.
C) habitual in.
D) shared by.

6.   My mother was sitting by the fire, but poorly in
health, and very low in spirits, looking at it through
her tears, and desponding heavily about herself and
the fatherless little stranger, who was already
5   welcomed by some grosses of prophetic pins, in a
drawer upstairs, to a world not at all excited on the
subject of his arrival; my mother, I say, was sitting by
the fire, that bright, windy March afternoon, very
timid and sad, and very doubtful of ever coming alive
10 out of the trial that was before her, when, lifting her
eyes as she dried them, to the window opposite, she
saw a strange lady coming up the garden.

6

As used in line 2, "low" most nearly means

A) stunted.
B) gloomy.
C) insignificant.
D) minor.

7.   Planetary scientists were surprised almost a
decade ago when they discovered that the most
plentiful types of meteorites they had collected and
studied on Earth were actually not common in space.
5   Now, a group of scientists has uncovered part of the
explanation. Mineralogical evidence in some
meteorites had already pointed to a cataclysmic
collision in the asteroid belt long before dinosaurs,
when multicellular animals were still fairly new.

7

As used in line 7, "pointed to" most nearly means

A) suggested.
B) preferred.
C) gestured.
D) diverted.

8.   One January day, thirty years ago, the little town
of Hanover, anchored on a windy Nebraska tableland,
was trying not to be blown away. A mist of fine
snowflakes was curling and eddying about the cluster
5 of low drab buildings huddled on the gray prairie,
under a gray sky. The dwelling-houses were set about
haphazard on the tough prairie sod; some of them
looked as if they had been moved in overnight, and
others as if they were straying off by themselves,
10 headed straight for the open plain.

8

As used in line 6, "set about" most nearly means

A) enveloped.
B) accumulated.
C) arranged.
D) ruined.

9.   It took hundreds of millions of years to produce
the life that now inhabits the earth eons of time in
which that developing and evolving and diversifying
life reached a state of adjustment and balance with its
5 surroundings. The environment, rigorously shaping
and directing the life it supported, contained elements
that were hostile as well as supporting. Certain rocks
gave out dangerous radiation; even within the
light of the sun, from which all life draws its energy,
10 there were short-wave radiations with power to injure.

9

As used in line 9, "draws" most nearly means

A) obtains.
B) restricts.
C) captivates.
D) lures.

10.   [Miss Bates] was a happy woman, and a woman
whom no one named without good-will. It was her
own universal good-will and contented temper which
worked such wonders. She loved every body, was
5 interested in every body's happiness, quicksighted to
every body's merits; thought herself a most fortunate
creature, and surrounded with blessings in such an
excellent mother, and so many good neighbours and
friends, and a home that wanted for nothing. The
10 simplicity and cheerfulness of her nature, her
contented and grateful spirit, were a recommendation
to every body, and a mine of felicity to herself.

10

As used in line 9, "wanted for" most nearly means

A) demanded.
B) lacked.
C) passed by.
D) overlooked.

Independent Practice: Set #2

1.　　　Systemic pesticides can be absorbed through roots and leaves and distributed throughout an entire plant, including pollen and nectar. These pesticides can poison bees directly, but even low-level exposure
5　to treated flowers can lead to damaging effects such as a compromised immune stem, altered learning, and impaired foraging, all of which have the result of making bees more vulnerable to infection.

1

As used in line 5, "treated" most nearly means

A) indulged.
B) affected.
C) improved.
D) repaired.

2.　　　[W]e are assembled to protest against a form of government existing without the consent of the governed—to declare our right to be free as man is free, to be represented in the government which we
5　are taxed to support, to have such disgraceful laws as give man the power to chastise and imprison his wife, to take the wages which she earns, the property which she inherits...We have met to uplift woman's fallen divinity upon an even pedestal with man's. And,
10　strange as it may seem to many, we now demand our right to vote according to the declaration of the government under which we live.

2

As used in line 9, "even" most nearly means

A) consistent.
B) equal.
C) parallel.
D) proportional.

3.　　　In tense situations, everything can change between beats of the heart. And, it's more than just the situation that changes—our own reaction to a potentially dangerous encounter can hang on
5　something as simple as the contraction of our heart. In a small study, researchers from the United Kingdom looked at how participant's perception of a threat changed with the beating of their hearts. They found that people were more likely to exhibit a reaction
10　based on fear when their hearts were pumping blood, as compared to the resting phase between heartbeats.

3

As used in line 4, "hang" most nearly means

A) lean.
B) bet.
C) depend.
D) focus.

4.   Mr. Woodhouse was fond of society in his own
way. He liked very much to have his friends come and
see him; and from various united causes, from his
long residence at Hartfield, and his good nature, from
5 his fortune, his house, and his daughter, he could
command the visits of his own little circle, in a great
measure, as he liked. He had not much intercourse
with any families beyond that circle; his horror of late
hours, and large dinner-parties, made him unfit for
10 any acquaintance but such as would visit him on his
own terms.

4

As used in line 6, "command" most nearly means

A) control.
B) charge.
C) prohibit.
D) announce.

5.   By using a new technique to study unhatched
dinosaur embryo fossils, scientists determined that
those embryos took twice as long to hatch as bird
eggs of a similar size. The embryo of a large duck-
5 billed dinosaur took at least six months to hatch, and
the eggs of larger dinosaurs may have taken even
longer. The long incubation times complicate thinking
about dinosaur behavior. While some kinds of
dinosaurs may have tended their eggs and young, for
10 others the difficulty of remaining in one place for
close to a year to watch buried eggs would have
proven impossible.

5

As used in line 9, "tended" most nearly means

A) abandoned.
B) considered.
C) drifted toward.
D) looked after.

6.   In fact, the only thing that appeared three-
dimensional about Boori Ma was her voice: brittle with
sorrows, as tart as curds, and shrill enough to grate meat
from a coconut. It was with this voice that she
5 enumerated, twice a day as she swept the stairwell, the
details of her plight and losses suffered since her
deportation to Calcutta after Partition. At that time, she
maintained, the turmoil had separated her from a
husband, four daughters, a two-story brick house, a
10 rosewood almari, and a number of coffer boxes whose
skeleton keys she still wore, along with their life savings,
tied to the free end of her sari.

6

As used in line 8, "maintained" most nearly means

A) supplied.
B) persevered.
C) proclaimed.
D) renewed.

7.　　　In a famous series of experiments on obedience
conducted by Stanford Professor Stanley Milgram in
the early 1960s, subjects were kept innocent of the
experiment's true purpose. Milgram cleverly informed
5　participants that he was testing the effects of
punishment on learning and memory. In reality, he was
testing factors that promote obedience to a person who
is perceived as a legitimate authority figure.

7

As used in line 3, "innocent" most nearly means

A) ignorant.
B) aware.
C) careless.
D) convinced.

8.　　　Numerous companies have embraced the open
office—about 70% of US offices are open concept —
and by most accounts, very few have moved back into
traditional spaces with offices and doors. But research
5　that we're 15% less productive, we have immense
trouble concentrating and we're twice as likely to get
sick in open working spaces, has contributed to a
growing backlash against open offices.

8

As used in line 1, "embraced" most nearly means

A) encircled.
B) seized.
C) adopted.
D) gripped.

9.　　　As an apology for addressing you, fellow-
citizens! we cannot announce the discovery of any
new principle adapted to ameliorate the condition of
mankind....We point to your principles, your wisdom,
5　and to your great example as the full justification of
our course this day. That "all men are created equal":
that "life, liberty, and the pursuit of happiness" are the
right of all; that "taxation and representation" should
go together; that governments are to protect, not to
10　destroy, the rights of mankind; that the Constitution of
the United States was formed to establish justice,
promote the general welfare, and secure the blessing
of liberty to all the people of this country...are
American principles and maxims, and together they
15　form and constitute the constructive elements of the
American government. From this elevated platform,
provided by the Republic for us, and for all the
children of men, we address you. In doing so, we
would have our spirit properly discerned.

9

As used in line 16, "elevated" most nearly means

A) raised.
B) lofty.
C) formal.
D) inflated.

10.   Miss Brooke had that kind of beauty which
     seems to be thrown into relief by poor dress. Her hand
     and wrist were so finely formed that she could wear
     sleeves not less bare of style than those in which the
5   Blessed Virgin appeared to Italian painters; and her
     profile as well as her stature and bearing seemed to
     gain the more dignity from her plain garments, which
     by the side of provincial fashion gave her the
     impressiveness of a fine quotation from the Bible—or
10   from one of our elder poets—in a paragraph of to-
     day's newspaper.

10

As used in line 3, "finely" most nearly means

A) solidly.
B) rarely.
C) ornately.
D) charmingly.

Answers: Vocabulary in Context Independent Practice

Set #1

1. C

The sentence following the one in which the word *shedding* appears refers to what scientists *now know* about meta-memory. Logically, the new study must be providing new information about how meta-memory works in the brain. The correct word must therefore be positive and mean something like "explaining" or "demonstrating." *Disposing* is negative, so B) can be eliminated immediately. Neither *adapting* nor *shimmering* means anything like "demonstrating," so A) and D) can be eliminated as well. That leaves *revealing*, which fits: a study that revealed how meta-memory worked would lead to new knowledge about meta-memory.

2. D

Think about the context provided by the passage: the biosensors are responsible for collecting and measuring huge amounts of data about how people's bodies behave over the course of a day. In other words, the biosensors are *monitoring* the bodies' behavior. A), *Stalking*, is far too negative, and *following* and *chasing* do not make sense at all, so B) and C) can also be eliminated. D) is thus correct.

3. A

Focus on the sentence in which the word *deeply* appears, particularly the information after the comma. (Remember to never just read half of a sentence!) What does it tell us? That interacting with different types of group members causes people to assume that agreement will not happen automatically (*reaching a consensus will take effort*). Logically, then, people participating in such groups must be more prepared than they would be otherwise. The correct word must therefore be positive and consistent with the idea of being well-prepared. D), *obscurely*, is negative, and B), *distantly*, does not make sense. Don't worry if you don't know the definition of C), *abysmally* (awfully). Instead, focus on *thoroughly*. Someone who is thoroughly prepared is someone more likely to *anticipate alternative viewpoints and expect that reaching a consensus will take effort*. A) is thus correct.

4. C

The sentence in which the word appears sets up a contrast between *the bottom* and *the highest round of success*, to which the narrator aims to rise. Picture someone climbing up a ladder or staircase, trying to reach the top. In that context, *round* must mean something like "level." *Aspect* doesn't really fit with that meaning, and neither does *procession*, so A) and B) can both be eliminated. Be careful with D): an *enclosure* is a space that's fenced in, like an animal's pen. That's not consistent with the idea of climbing up to the top of something. In contrast, a *rung* is a step on a ladder—the highest rung is something that a person rising up would aim to reach. C) is thus correct.

5. D

The phrase *occupies the space agencies of nations around the world* indicates that the "dream" of exploring the solar system is something that countries around the world have in common. In other words, it is *shared by* them. None of the other answers creates a logical meaning when plugged into the sentence, so D) is correct.

6. B

 The sentence in which the word *low* appears also refers to the mother's poor health and tears. Based on those references, it's clear that she's pretty sad, so the correct answer must be consistent with the idea of negative feelings. *Gloomy* = sad, making B) correct. A), *Stunted* (underdeveloped), and D), *minor*, cannot really be used to describe emotions, and C), *insignificant*, does not make sense: negative emotions can still be quite significant.

7. A

The previous sentence refers to an *explanation*, and the sentence that contains *pointed to* serves to expand on that explanation. In that context, *pointed to* must mean something like "indicated" or "revealed." *Preferred* and *gestured* do not make any sense in context; in addition, "gestured" is the literal meaning of *pointed to*, which suggests that this answer is incorrect. B) and C) can thus be eliminated. D), *diverted*, does not make sense either: the passage is talking about collisions that <u>did</u> occur, and *diverted* would imply that a collision was avoided. *Suggested* is the only option consistent with the idea of an explanation, so A) is correct.

8. C

The phrase *some of them looked as if they had been moved in overnight, and others as if they were straying off by themselves* describes how the houses were *arranged* on the prairie, so C) is the clearest fit. There is nothing in the passage to suggest that the houses were *enveloped* (enclosed) or *ruined*. *Accumulated* simply does not make sense. All of the other answers can thus be eliminated.

9. A

Unfortunately, this passage does not provide any specific words or phrases that correspond to the answer; rather, you must determine the correct word based on the general context. Logically, the relationship between light and life must be a positive one: you might plug in a word like *gets*. *Restricts* is negative, so B) can be eliminated. *Lures* has a negative connotation as well: usually, it's used to refer to drawing someone into a trap. D) can thus be eliminated. *Captivates* (enchants) doesn't make sense either, so C) can also be eliminated. That leaves A). *Obtains* fits as a synonym for *gets* and correctly conveys the positive relationship between light and life.

10. B

The passage focuses on how fortunate Miss Bates is, and on the many things that she has (*a most fortunate creature, and surrounded with blessings*). Given the implication that the woman has everything, it is reasonable to assume that her home "wants for," i.e. *lacks*, nothing. Otherwise, think of it this way: a home cannot *demand, pass by,* or *overlook* anything; only people can do those things.

Shortcut: know that "lack" is a common second meaning of *want (for)*.

Set #2

1. B

The passage focuses on pesticides that are harmful to bees (*damaging effects such as compromised immune system...impaired foraging*, etc.), so *treated* cannot have a positive meaning. *Indulged* (gave into), *improved*, and *repaired* are all clearly positive, eliminating A), C), and D). *Affected* can have a negative connotation, and this word also fits the passage: flowers treated with pesticides are by definition affected by them. B) is thus correct.

2. B

The key phrase in this passage comes in the previous sentence (which is admittedly very long): the author declares the goal of being *as free as man is free*. In other words, the goal is to be *equal*. Given that context, B) is the only answer that makes sense.

3. C

The passage indicates that fear reactions are more likely to occur when hearts are pumping than when they are resting. In other words, people's reactions to potentially dangerous encounters *depend* on what their hearts are doing at the time of the encounter. C) is thus correct. The other answers do not make sense in context.

4. A

The last sentence contains the key information, but it is presented in a potentially confusing way. The phrase *unfit for any acquaintance but such as would visit him on his own terms* means that the only acquaintances Mr. Woodhouse had were those who would visit him on his own terms. This information indicates that Mr. Woodhouse wanted to be able to direct, or *control*, his visits with friends. A) is thus correct. B), *charge*, and D), *announce*, do not fit at all, and C), *prohibit*, is too strong: the passage indicates only that Mr. Woodhouse wanted control over his socializing; he did not want to prevent visits from his own friends.

5. D

The last sentence contrasts the behavior of dinosaurs that *tended their eggs and young*, with the behavior or dinosaurs that could not *remain in one place to watch buried eggs*. The correct word must therefore be positive and mean something like "watched" or "cared for." *Abandoned* is negative and means exactly the opposite of what is required, eliminating A). *Considered* and *drifted toward* are not the same thing as caring for, so B) and C) can be eliminated as well. Only *looked after* is consistent with the idea of caring for, making D) correct.

6. C

The key information is in the previous two sentences, which focus on Boori Ma's *voice* and all the terrible experiences she uses it to describe. Given that context, *maintain* must have something to do with telling *the details of her plight. Supplied, persevered*, and *renewed* are in no way synonyms for *telling*, but *proclaiming* fits and is consistent with the idea of loudly complaining. C) is thus correct.

7. A

The passage indicates that Milgram hid the true purpose of the experiment from the subjects: he led them to believe that he was testing the effects of punishment on learning, but really he was testing obedience to authority figures. Based on that information, it is clear that the subjects did not know the true purpose of the experiment—that is, they were *ignorant of it*. A) is thus correct. B), *aware*, and D), *convinced*, imply the opposite of the required word. C), *careless*, does not make sense at all.

8. C

The passage states that *70% of US offices are open concept*, indicating that many offices have implemented or accepted the open concept model. Clearly, the correct word must be positive. *Seized* is negative, so B) can be eliminated. *Encircled* means "surrounded," which does not make sense, so A) can be crossed out as well. D), *gripped*, does not fit either. Only *adopted* is both positive and consistent with the idea of implementing a new model, making C) correct.

9. B

Throughout the passage, the author (Frederick Douglass) invokes high-minded, abstract principles involving governmental rights and responsibilities (*life, liberty, and the pursuit of happiness…the Constitution of the United Sates was formed to establish justice, promote the general welfare, and secure the blessing of liberty*). The word most consistent with that kind of high-mindedness is *lofty*. It indicates that Douglass is not talking about platform that is literally raised off the ground, but rather one that is intended to evoke grand ideals and principles. *Raised* is too literal, and *inflated* is too negative, eliminating A) and D). *Formal* does not capture the connotation of high-mindedness that is present throughout the passage, eliminating C) as well.

10. D

The key information appears in the first sentence, which announces the topic of the passage: Miss Brooke's *beauty*. As a result, the correct word must mean something like "beautifully." *Solidly* and *rarely* do not make sense at all, so A) and B) can be eliminated. Be careful with C): *ornate* means "decorated," and it would not make any sense to say that a person's wrists were formed in a decorated way. *Charmingly* is consistent with the idea of beauty and is a much more direct fit. D) is thus correct.

Glossary of Common Second Meanings

Account (for) – explain

Affect (v.) – to adopt (a behavior); affected (adj.) – behaving in an artificial/pretentious way

Afford – grant (e.g. an opportunity)

Arrangement – situation

Arrest – put a stop to (not just put handcuffs on a criminal)

Assume – take on responsibility for, acquire (e.g. to assume a new position)

Basic – essential, fundamental

Becoming (adj.) – fitting, flattering

Bent – liking or preference for

Boost – improve, promote

Calculated – plotted out

Capacity – ability

Chance (v.) – attempt

Check – control (e.g. *The vaccine checked the spread of the disease*)

Clear – obvious, unmistakable

Coin (v.) – invent (e.g. coin a phrase)

Common – shared

Compromise (v.) – endanger or make vulnerable (e.g. to compromise one's beliefs)

Constitution – build (e.g. a football player has a solid constitution)

Conviction – strong belief (noun form of *convinced*)

Couch (v.) – hide

Critical – essential, necessary

Curious – odd

Currency – acceptance, approval (of an idea)

Direct (v.) – guide

Discriminating – perceptive

Disposed – inclined

Distant – aloof, emotionally uninvolved

Doctor (v.) – tamper with, alter

Draw (v.) - attract

Economy – thrift (e.g. a writer who has an *economical* style is one who uses few words)

Embroider – falsify, make up stories about

Establish – demonstrate, confirm

Exchange (n.) – conversation

Execute – carry out

Exploit – make use of, take advantage of (does not carry a negative connotation)

Facility – talent for

Fierce – intense

Fine – (1) keen, perceptive; (2) well-developed

Foil – to put a stop to (e.g. to foil a robbery)

Foundation – basis, underpinning

Grand – imposing

Grave/Gravity – serious(ness)

Great – large

Harbor – To possess, hold (e.g. to harbor a belief)

Hold – claim

Hold out – resist

Host – contain

Independent – separate (e.g. an independent variable)

Modest – small, limited (e.g. a modest amount = a small amount)

Nature – type

Observe – follow (e.g. a law)

Open – accessible

Peculiar (to) – unique, distinctive

Plastic/plasticity – able to be changed

Poor – weak (e.g. a performance)

Provoke – elicit (e.g. a reaction)

Put (v.) – state, say

Qualify – provide more information or detail about

Raise (v.) – (1) rear (e.g. an animal); (2) elevate/uplift

Range – scope

Raw – unfiltered

Realize – achieve (a goal)

Reconcile – bring together

Regular – even

Relate/Relay - pass on information, give an account of (a story)

Reservations – misgivings

Reserve – hold off on (e.g. to reserve judgment)

Ripple (v.) – spread

Ruffled – flustered, anxious (unruffled – calm)

Sap (v.) – drain (e.g. of energy)

Scour – search

Scrap (v.) – eliminate

Set – determine

Sheer – pure, simple

Shelve/Table (v.) – reject or discard (e.g. an idea or proposal)

Simple – straightforward

Sober – serious, modest

Sound – firm, stable, reliable, valid (e.g. a sound argument)

Spare, Severe – plain, unadorned

Splinter (v.) – split off

State - condition

Static – unchanging (i.e. in a state of *stasis*)

Station – rank

Scale – level

Store (n.) – reserve

Sustain (v.) – withstand

Temper (v.) – moderate, make less harsh

Tied (to) – connected to

Train (v.) – fixate on (e.g. *train* one's eyes on something)

Track – follow

True – genuine

Uniform – constant, unvarying

Unqualified – absolute

Upset (v.) – interfere with an expected outcome

Urge – advocate, be in favor of

Values – principles

Wake – aftermath

Want – lack

Yield – reveal (e.g. an experiment yields results)

Chapter 2: Passage-Based Vocabulary

Which part of the SAT worries you the most: the Reading Test, the Writing and Language Test, or the Math Test? Many students answer without hesitation, "The Reading Test!" The reasons for their concern are not hard to find. The SAT Reading Test gives you 65 minutes to read five passages and answer 52 questions. Both the passages and the questions contain a challenging array of vocabulary words.

This chapter provides you with definitions and examples of 50 words that have played a key role on the new SAT. You will not be asked to define these words directly. Instead, you will be asked to apply them in a variety of Reading Test questions. This chapter is designed to teach you a carefully sequenced set of skills that will help you improve your Reading Test score.

SAT passages can be grouped into three categories. The first passage is always drawn from a work of American or world literature, either classic (typically nineteenth century) or contemporary. In addition, there are always three science passages that focus on topics drawn from the social, physical, and natural sciences. These passages are primarily excerpted from recent articles that have appeared in "serious" mainstream magazines such as *Time*, *Scientific American*, or *Smithsonian*. And finally, there will always be a history passage, or passages—what the College Board refers to as "The Great Global Conversation." This reading often takes the form of a dual passage in which two authors express different viewpoints about topics such as the role of women in a democracy or the response of citizens to unjust laws.

Vocabulary plays an important role in a number of the 52 questions that accompany the five Reading Test passages, not just in terms of the vocabulary-in-context questions covered in the previous chapter. This chapter will focus on questions in which your knowledge of key groups of vocabulary words will increase your ability to select correct answers.

Our careful analysis of the Reading Test passages and questions reveals that each of the three types of passages generates a distinctive set of vocabulary words. In the following pages, we define and illustrate the key words from each of these three sets, listed in approximate order of importance. We conclude with practice questions designed to enhance your ability to correctly answer Reading Test questions utilizing key vocabulary words.

Natural and Social Science

Each science passage describes the aims, methods, and results of a scientific investigation. As a result, these passages and their accompanying questions all employ a distinctive vocabulary that focuses on the language of evidence and experimentation.

In the section below, we define 25 of these key words and illustrate how College Board test-writers use and test them. We will also provide helpful tips that will enable you to save time by going directly to the correct answer.

1. Hypothesis – a proposed insight or explanation

A **hypothesis** is a proposed insight that has not been tested or verified. Science passages typically begin with a **hypothesis** that is then revised, challenged, strengthened, and sometimes confirmed. In one passage, for example, chemical ecologists **hypothesized** that enhancing the scent of Texas gourd flowers would attract more desired squash bees while repelling unwanted striped cucumber beetles. To their surprise, squash bees were indifferent to the fragrance-enhanced blossoms. This unexpected finding forced the chemical ecologists to revise their **hypothesis**.

2. Empirical – derived from experiment and observation

Empirical evidence is data derived from experiments and observations rather than from abstract theories. The chemical ecologists described in the previous example tested their hypothesis by conducting a carefully controlled experiment in which they collected **empirical** data from 168 Texas gourd vines. Scientists are reluctant to accept a hypothesis when **empirical** information is not available. For instance, a passage on the Higgs Boson explains that the scientific community initially rejected Higgs's ideas because they rested on speculation and not on **empirical** evidence.

3. Central claim – primary assertion

College Board test-writers frequently use the phrase **central claim**. This phrase appears often in questions, which may ask you to identify a **central claim** supported by data in a table. Don't let this phrase confuse you. *Central* means "main" or "primary," and a *claim* is an argument. So a **central claim** = the main argument or hypothesis discussed in a passage.

4. Counterclaim – counterargument

A **counterclaim** is a counterargument made to rebut (argue against) a claim discussed previously in the passage. Science passages often include a **counterclaim** posed by a dissenting scientist—that is, a scientist who rejects the main theory discussed in the passage. For example, in a passage about the origins of tectonic plates, one geochemist contended that the rocks studied by other geochemists were too old and deformed to provide reliable data.

5. Hypothetical – theoretical, based on speculation

Hypothetical describes an idea or situation that only exists as a theoretical concept. For example, time travel is a **hypothetical** phenomenon: it could exist, but right now it is only possible in science fiction movies. Although they are not real, **hypothetical** situations can challenge scientists to explore new hypotheses about puzzling natural phenomena.

6. Irreconcilable – unresolvable

What do celebrity magazines and SAT science passages have in common? Both frequently use the word **irreconcilable** to describe differences that cannot be resolved. Celebrity magazines often feature sensational accounts describing how **irreconcilable** differences are responsible for movie stars' breakups. SAT science passages provide scholarly accounts of seemingly **irreconcilable** hypotheses. For example, the passage about the Higgs Boson explained why the Higgs Field enabled physicists to reconcile two seemingly **irreconcilable** phenomena—that is, it explained why two seemingly contradictory phenomena could actually exist at the same time.

7. Context – the setting or background information

Context refers to the setting or frame of reference necessary to understand a topic. Knowing the **context** enables you to place an issue in a broader perspective. Our examination of the released tests reveals a surprising and helpful pattern: there is a 50 % chance that your Reading Test will include an answer choice featuring the word **context**. So far, there is a 100% chance that this choice will be the correct answer!

8. Consensus – general agreement

A **consensus** is a general agreement about an idea or theory. Science passages often begin with a hypothesis that enjoys a widespread **consensus**. For example, in one passage we learn that neuroscientists long believed that the adult human brain was incapable of spawning new neurons. However, a groundbreaking study of London taxi drivers revealed that this **consensus** view was inaccurate.

9. Fundamental – basic and essential

Fundamental is a frequently used descriptive word meaning "basic" or "essential." For example, the phrase "the brain's **fundamental** anatomical structure" describes the brain's basic structure.

10. Yield – to produce or generate

When you are driving, the word **yield** means "to give up the right of way." But when you are reading an SAT science passage, **yield** means "to produce, provide, or generate." For example, most science passages include a table that **yields** evidence that may support, modify, or even weaken a hypothesis.

11. Emphasize and Elaborate – to stress and fully develop

The phrase **emphasize and elaborate** is often used to summarize research findings. **Emphasize** means "to accentuate or single out," and **elaborate** means "to develop additional details." A scientist who **emphasizes** and **elaborates** on a hypothesis will often clarify what was initially a puzzling finding.

12. Underscore – to emphasize

Has one of your teachers ever written a key term on the whiteboard and then emphatically drawn a line under it? If so, you have witnessed a dramatic and hopefully effective illustration of why **underscore** means "emphasize." It is important to note that SAT science passages rarely include an **underscored** word or phrase. However, they sometimes include an italicized word or phrase that is intended to **underscore** a key fact, idea, or claim.

13. **Undermine** – to weaken or damage

Look closely at the word **undermine**. It literally means, "to dig under a mine and therefore weaken it." A scientist who **undermines** a hypothesis or argument is attempting to weaken it. For example, experimental data can sometimes be used to **undermine** a claim.

14. **Detrimental** – very harmful

The prefix DE- signals that **detrimental** is a negative word describing a situation or action in which things are literally going down. In fact, **detrimental** means "going down" in the sense of causing damage or harm. For example, in one passage proponents of organic farming argue that conventional agriculture produces fruits and vegetables that are **detrimental** to the environment. (**Note:** In the past, SAT prep books recommended that students learn long lists of prefixes. Our analysis reveals that this is no longer necessary. So far, DE- is the only prefix you need to know.)

15. **Optimistic** – confident of a positive outcome; **Pessimistic** – confident of a negative outcome

Optimistic is a straightforward word that always describes a hopeful, confident, and even cheerful outlook. For example, a passage on the solar panel industry highlighted the work of leading researchers who are **optimistic** about the long-term prospects of using solar panels to lower energy costs. It is important to note that not all solar panel experts are **optimistic**. The passage also noted that some experts are **pessimistic**, or discouraged, because weak market conditions are eroding profits and slowing innovation.

16. **Incongruous** – incompatible, obviously inconsistent with a particular situation

What do a New York Yankees baseball hat, a Boston Red Sox jacket, and the planet Jupiter have in common? They all illustrate the word **incongruous**. Let us explain: Larry often wears his favorite Yankees baseball hat AND his favorite Boston Red Sox jacket. This **incongruous** combination confuses people who point out that the two teams are bitter rivals. How can he simultaneously be a fan of the Yankees and the Red Sox? Although the combination is indeed **incongruous**, the hat and the jacket are comfortable, and that is all that matters to him. Planetary astronomers are not concerned with **incongruous** sportswear, but they are concerned with **incongruities** in space. For example, planetary scientists in one recent passage noted the **incongruity** between their knowledge of water on distant planets and their lack of knowledge about the amount of water on nearby Jupiter. The **incongruity** is explained by the fact that Jupiter is so cold that all the water sinks into the planet, far out of sight.

17. **Enumerate** – to list

Enumerate literally means to "numerate" or number things in a list. For example, in the *Declaration of Independence*, Thomas Jefferson **enumerates** a long list of colonial grievances (complaints) against King George III. While SAT science passages do not **enumerate** grievances, they often do **enumerate** the advantages of a program or innovation. For example, the author of the passage about solar panels **enumerated** several advantages of this new technology.

18. **Tentative** – undecided, not certain

Tentative means "undecided." Science passages often use moderating words and phrases such as *perhaps* and *at first glance* to indicate that a theory is **tentative**. For example, a passage about the duckbill dinosaur indicates that paleontologists initially expressed a **tentative** understanding of the function of this prehistoric creature's distinctive but puzzling head ornamentation.

19. **Analogy** – a comparison between two dissimilar ideas or objects

Science writers are frequently faced with the problem of describing very abstract concepts. They often solve this problem by using **analogies** to compare unfamiliar ideas or objects to familiar ones. For example, one writer faced the difficult task of describing how the Higgs field exerts a drag force on particles when they accelerate through the field. The author used a clever but simple **analogy** in which he asked readers to "think of a ping pong ball submerged in water." He then pointed out that if you push on the ping pong ball, it "will feel much more massive than it does outside of water."

20. **Analogous** – characterized by a parallel similarity

Analogous is the noun form of *analogy*. It is used to describe two similar situations between which a comparison can be drawn. For example, one challenging question asked test-takers to use a graph to identify a historic example in the mid-1980s that was "most analogous to" a hypothetical situation in another time period. Simply stated, this question asked students to identify a condition or scenario that was most similar to an event in the mid-1980s.

21. **Approximation** – an estimate

Although scientists strive to be as exact as possible, they nonetheless must often begin with an **approximation**, or estimate. For example, in a comparative study of dogs and wolves, scientists initially speculated that wolves raised by humans would demonstrate social-cognitive skills **approximating** those of dogs raised by humans.

22. **Innate** – inborn

The scientists who studied the social-cognitive differences between dogs and wolves (see above) ultimately concluded that **innate** or inborn differences account for many of the different behaviors between the two species.

23. **Underlying Assumption** – a basic belief that is not directly stated

Underlying literally refers to something lying beneath something else; however, the word **underlying** can have a subtler meaning. In SAT science passages, an **underlying assumption** refers to a basic belief that is present but not directly stated in the passage. For example, the **underlying assumption** in a study of dogs and wolves was that innate genetic differences would account for the difference in their behaviors.

24. **Haphazard** – random

Have you ever looked at the nighttime sky? At first glance, the stars and galaxies appear to be spread across the heavens in a **haphazard**, or random, manner. However, in recent years some astronomers have begun to question this long-held assumption. For example, in a recent science passage, Margaret Geller contends that advanced maps of the known universe reveal a remarkable pattern that resembles a gigantic stickman.

25. **Adept** – very skillful

What do the fictional superhero Captain America and the scientists in a typical SAT Reading Test passage have in common? Both are very **adept**, or skillful, at accomplishing their goals. Captain America is **adept** at defeating villains who want to overwhelm the Avengers and conquer Earth. The scientists featured in SAT science passages are very **adept** at formulating and testing hypotheses.

Historical Documents

SAT Reading Tests always include passages drawn from significant historical documents ("The Great Global Conversation"). These passages focus on questions of freedom, justice, and human rights, and they consist of excerpts from well-known articles and speeches by both American and international authors. These excerpts are often combined into dual passages, which frequently present conflicting points of view on a topic. These passages also contain a very distinctive vocabulary. All 15 of the following words have generated answers on recent tests.

26. **Subordinate** – lower in rank, occupying an inferior position

Look closely at the word **subordinate**. SUB- means "lower" or "under," and ORDINATE refers to an order of things. So **subordinate** describes a lower or inferior position. In an essay published in 1837, Catherine Beecher argued, "Heaven has appointed to one sex the superior, and to the other the **subordinate** station." It is important to note that although Beecher believed that women occupy a "**subordinate** relation" to men, she also argued that women could play a significant role in society by exerting influence within their homes and families.

27. **Station** – position or rank

What do you think of when you hear the word **station**? Most people would probably respond by saying "a gas station" or "a train station." While **station** can refer to a stopping place for cars and trains, it can also refer to a position or rank someone occupies in society. In the example above, Catherine Beecher argues that women are assigned a subordinate **station**, or lower rank.

28. **Peculiar** – distinctive

The word **peculiar** normally refers to unusual or strange behavior. It can even describe an odd odor. During the nineteenth century, authors like Catherine Beecher used **peculiar** to mean "distinctive." That is why she wrote that the power of women "should be altogether different and **peculiar**" from that of men." It is also interesting to note that Southern defenders of slavery referred to the practice as "our peculiar institution." In their view, the word **peculiar** did not mean odd or strange. Instead, it referred to something distinctive about or characteristic of the Southern way of life.

29. **Sarcastic** – using irony to mock or convey contempt

Richard Price was a British political philosopher who criticized King George III's decision to use force to subdue the thirteen North American colonies. In an essay excerpted by the College Board, Price scornfully points out that the King and Parliament have convinced themselves that the colonists will be "much happier under our government than under any government of their own." He then **sarcastically** asks, "How kind is it thus to take upon us the trouble of judging for them what is most for their happiness?" The word *kind* conveys Price's **sarcastic**, or mocking, tone.

30. **Degrade** – to deteriorate, to lower in dignity

As we have noted in Word #14 above, the prefix DE- signals that things are going down. **Degrade** means "deteriorate" in the sense of lowering in quality or value. In a passage about the social and political roles of men and women, the nineteenth century French writer Alexis de Tocqueville contended that by "attempting to make one sex equal to the other, both are **degraded**." He goes on to insist that this will produce "weak men and disorderly women." Your knowledge of **degraded** should enable you to conclude that de Tocqueville believed that extending political and social rights to women would harm both sexes.

31. Entrenched – deeply established

The College Board did not allow de Tocqueville's views to stand uncontested. De Tocqueville's passage was part of a dual reading that also included a passage by the British philosopher Harriet Taylor Mill. A contemporary of de Tocqueville, Mill contended that inequality had been deeply **entrenched**, or long established, for generations. **Entrenched** literally means "to surround by a strong defensive trench." When Mill wrote in the early 1850s, both women and enslaved Africans faced deeply **entrenched** systems of inequality.

32. Tenacious – persistent and determined

Harriet Mill was not a naïve idealist. She recognized that the strong emotions surrounding existing social roles would be **tenacious** and was thus persistent and determined in her defense of women's equality.

33. Dominion – supremacy

Dominion means "characterized by supremacy and dominance." Harriet Mill argued for "a just equality instead of what she called "the **dominion**" of the strongest. She believed that gender roles would change because of an ongoing social shift toward greater equality. This inevitable movement would enable both men and women to achieve their full potential.

34. Revere – to show deep respect

Cesar Chavez is now **revered** as an iconic American labor leader and civil rights activist. The deep respect for Chavez can be seen in the many schools, streets, and parks named after him. The College Board recognized America's great respect for Chavez by devoting a dual passage to his role in leading the historic Delano strike.

35. Disparity – inequality

Look closely at the word **disparity**. The Latin root PAR- means "equal." That's why when golfers are par for a course, they are literally equal to the course. So **parity** means "equal to." In contrast, **disparity** signals an inequality. Led by Cesar Chavez, farm workers in California protested the **disparity** between the working conditions of nonunion farm workers and unionized industrial workers.

36. Antagonism – strong opposition

Chavez recognized that the farm workers faced a long and uphill struggle. A deep **antagonism**, or strong opposition, divided the farm workers and the growers. Influenced by Martin Luther King, Chavez believed that non-violent protests would garner national support and eventually erode the **antagonism** between the farm workers and the growers.

37. Repudiate – to reject

Should you always obey the law? The College Board explored this issue in a dual passage containing excerpts from writings by Abraham Lincoln and Henry David Thoreau. Lincoln contended that allowing people to break laws would **repudiate**, or reject, America's core value of respect for the law. However, Lincoln did not say that there are no unjust laws. He emphasized that "bad laws" should be followed until they are changed by "proper legal provisions."

38. **Advocate** – to publicly recommend, to urge

Lincoln's policy of restraint (see Word #37) did not convince Henry David Thoreau. Thoreau **advocated**, or urged, that his fellow Americans break any law forcing them to be "the agent of injustice."

39. **Discredited** – damaged and disgraced

The renowned African American abolitionist leader Frederick Douglass applied Thoreau's critique of unjust laws to slavery. In a famous speech excerpted by the College Board, Douglass argued that slavery was a **discredited**, or disgraced, institution because it violated America's principles of liberty, justice, and equality.

40. **Populist** – a person who identifies with ordinary people

American history contains a number of noteworthy examples of **populists** who identified with the concerns of ordinary people. In a dual passage, the College Board featured an 1828 Independence Day address delivered by Francis Wright. The speech emphasized that Wright was a **populist** who eloquently expressed her "love of the public good" and her "preference for the interests of the many to those of the few."

American and World Literature

In the past, literature passages often tested rhetorical devices such as paradox, personification, and metaphorical language. Thus far, the new SAT has not tested your knowledge of this type of vocabulary. Instead, questions focus on vocabulary in context (see Chapter 1), comprehension, and descriptive words and phrases. The section will define and illustrate how 10 vocabulary words and phrases have been used on recent exams.

41. Earnest – marked by deep sincerity and serious intent

How can you determine whether someone has an **earnest** attitude? In his song "Watcha Say," Jason Derulo readily acknowledges that he should have treated his girlfriend better. He then **earnestly** begs her to "give me another chance to be your man." SAT Reading Test passages are subtler than Jason's heartfelt plea. For example, in an excerpt from the novel *Portrait in Sepia*, we meet a young girl who is bright but aimless. She then receives a beautiful Kodak camera. The young girl tells us, "I picked it up with reverence." The word **reverence** (see Word #34) means "great respect." This signals the young girl's **earnest** interest in learning how to use her new camera.

42. Indifferent – characterized by a lack of interest or concern

Indifferent characters are easily recognized by their lack of interest in a topic. For example, in the short story "Nawabdin Election," the laborer Nawabdin comes to his boss, K.K. Harouni, to explain that he is no longer able to ride his bicycle as easily as he could as a younger man. The narrator states that Harouni "didn't particularly care one way or the other, except that it touched on his [own] comfort." In other words, Harouni was largely **indifferent** to Nawabdin's plight.

43. Diligent – careful and conscientious

Diligent describes someone who is careful and conscientious. It is a trait that employers value. But how can an employee demonstrate that he or she is **diligent**? To return to the example of "Nawabdin Election," the hardworking Nawabdin devises a clever way to prove to his boss that he is indeed a **diligent** worker. Rather than reciting a list of his accomplishments, Nawabdin bows his head, revealing a collection of gray hairs. The demonstration works, and the boss awards Newabdin a highly prized new motorcycle.

44. Dismissive – showing disregard and a lack of interest

Body language can provide a revealing insight into someone's true feelings. For example, in *Brewster: A Novel*, a track coach admonishes a novice runner named Mosher to pace himself and avoid "doing anything stupid." But eager to prove himself to his teammates, Mosher just shrugs his shoulders. The description of Mosher's body language underscores his **dismissive** attitude towards his coach's advice.

45. Arrant – complete and total

Arrant is an adjective that intensifies the word it modifies. For example, **arrant** nonsense means "total nonsense." In *The Amazing Adventures of Kavalier & Clay*, the narrator describes a pivotal moment when Rosa Saxon suddenly understands "the true horror of her destiny, the **arrant** purposelessness of her life." The use of **arrant** emphasizes the emptiness in Rosa's life.

46. Flush – a sudden rush of intense emotion

Flush typically describes a cleaning action that uses water. For example, ophthalmologists **flush** your eyes, and everyone has **flushed** a toilet. However, **flush** can also be used to describe a sudden rush of intense emotion. For example, in the passage described in Word #45, Rosa Saxon accepts a proposal to become a full-time cartoonist "with a **flush** of gratitude." The phrase "**flush** of gratitude" provides a vivid way of conveying Rosa's excitement at beginning a new career.

47. Vitality – filled with energy

What do the British-American rock band Katrina and the Waves and the fictional character Eppie in George Eliot's novel *Silas Marner* have in common? Both exhibit a distinctive energy and **vitality**. Katrina enjoys a special feeling of "walking on sunshine" when she is with her boyfriend. Eppie is an adorable child who delights in "loving sunshine and living sounds." On a recent SAT, these traits clearly supported linking Eppie with the word **vitality**.

48. Despondent – very sad and discouraged

Despondent describes a feeling that is very different than the exuberant **vitality** exhibited by young Eppie Marner (see Word #47). The prefix DE- signals that this is a "down" word. In his classic song "What Becomes of the Broken-hearted?" a **despondent** Jimmy Ruffin describes himself as "filled with sadness" as he asks, "What becomes of the broken-hearted, who had love that's now departed?" SAT literary passages sometimes include characters who, like Jimmy Ruffin, feel **despondent** because they have suffered great losses.

49. Mar – to spoil and thus render less perfect

Mar is a straightforward negative word meaning "to spoil or damage and thus render less perfect." For example, Mark Zuckerberg's neighbors on the Hawaiian island of Kauai are accusing the Facebook founder of building a six-foot high wall that is **marring** their view of the Pacific Ocean. It is a long way from Mark Zuckerberg's wall to an illustration of **mar** on a recent Reading Test. The exam began with an excerpt from *The Emperor of Ocean Park* by Stephen L. Carter. The narrator opens his story by telling us that his sister Mariah was "touchingly devoted to the impossible work of gaining their [parents'] approval." The key phrase "impossible work" provides evidence that Mariah's relationship with her parents is **marred** by their excessive demands.

50. Solemn – serious and dignified

Have you ever attended a funeral? If so, then you know that the mood is **solemn**, or serious and dignified. A recent Reading Test passage described callers at the funeral as being "formal and sober." This phrase provides evidence that the funeral was a **solemn** event.

Characteristics of Correct Answers: Same Idea, Different Words

Identifying correct answers is the only way to earn points on the Reading Test. So what are the characteristics of a correct answer? Let's begin your quest for correct answers with the following paragraph and question:

The efforts by women to gain equality in the scientific workplace began in the early twentieth century. The women who began undertaking careers in science had little support from any part of the
5 society in which they lived. They had to struggle alone against a male-dominated scientific community. Even talented female scientists were forced to accept subordinate roles as assistants in large bureaucratic organizations. As a result, they had little voice in
10 making key decisions.

1

What point does the author make about the status of aspiring female scientists in the early twentieth century?

A) They were more ambitious than their male counterparts.
B) They had more rights than their male counterparts.
C) They depended upon men for their safety and job security.
D) They were forced to accept subordinate roles as assistants.

Did you have any trouble finding the correct answer? Probably not. Choice D) provides the correct answer by giving you a direct quote from the passage.

Now, reread the paragraph and answer the following question:

The efforts by women to gain equality in the scientific workplace began in the early twentieth century. The women who began undertaking careers in science had little support from any part of the
5 society in which they lived. They had to struggle alone against a male-dominated scientific community. Even talented female scientists were forced to accept subordinate roles as assistants in large bureaucratic organizations. As a result, they had little voice in
10 making key decisions.

1

What point does the author make about the status of aspiring female scientists in the early twentieth century?

A) They were more ambitious than their male counterparts.
B) They had more rights than their male counterparts.
C) They depended upon men for their safety and job security.
D) They were compelled to accept inferior roles.

As you can see, the question here is identical to the one above, with the exception of Choice D). Although choice D) is worded differently, it is still correct. The phrase *compelled to accept inferior roles* is a restatement of the textual statement *forced to accept subordinate* (see Word #26) *roles as assistants*. *Compelled* = forced, *inferior* = subordinate. Same idea, different words.

The Golden Rule: The Answer is in the Passage

The example above illustrates an extremely important rule: every SAT Reading Test question has just one objective answer that restates relevant ideas or information from the passage. Always remember this golden rule when you are answering passage-based questions: **the answer is the answer because it is supported by the passage**. This support will take the form of key words, phrases, and examples. Never, ever go outside the passage to find support for your answers.

A Sophisticated Game of Verbal Matching

Since correct answers are restatements of information from the passage, your job is to match key ideas from the text with their accurate restatements in each set of answers. In effect, the College Board is asking you to play a sophisticated game of verbal matching. The exercises below are designed to help you begin the process of recognizing the types of paraphrases you will encounter on the Reading Test.

In the following two exercises, match the passage phrases in the left column with answer restatements in the right column. (Answers p. 52)

Practice Set #1

1. _____ insufficient support	A. scattered haphazardly
2. _____ it had long been thought	B. weak evidence
3. _____ hopeful about the future	C. little empirical basis
4. _____ extensive speculation	D. question a consensus
5. _____ distributed at random	E. optimistic going forward

Practice Set #2

1. _____ remain tentative	A. necessarily innate
2. _____ retard commerce	B. open people's thoughts
3. _____ attributable to genetics	C. great disparities
4. _____ immense distance	D. endanger economic prosperity
5. _____ enlarge all minds	E. still unsettled

Questions From Paragraphs

Paragraphs are units of thought. As a result of this important organizational fact, many Reading Test questions are anchored in specific paragraphs. The following three paragraphs and their accompanying questions are designed to give you practice matching key passage words and phrases with question answers. Our explanations follow each question.

Practice Paragraph #1

I don't know why I thought Mama Day would be a big, tall woman. From the stories you told about your clashes with her, she had loomed that way in my mind. Hard. Strong. Yes, it definitely showed in the
5 set of her shoulders. But she was barely five feet and could have been snapped in the middle with one good-sized hand…"I'm Mama Day to some, Miss Miranda to others. You decide what I'll be to you." That type of straightforward honesty would cheapen
10 anyone less than the same."

1

The narrator's primary impression of Mama Day is that she is

A) noisy but distracting.
B) small but arrogant.
C) like a character from a history book.
D) both forceful and forthright.

The correct answer is D). Mama Day is best described as "forceful" because she is *Hard* and *Strong*. She is best described as "forthright" because of her *straightforward honesty*. Choice B) is tricky. It is true that Mama Day is small, but there is no support to justify describing her as arrogant. Choices A) and C) are entirely unsupported by the passage.

Practice Paragraph #2

Ninety-five percent of Greenland is covered by ice. Towns and villages cling to the coastline; at their backs loom glaciers a thousand meters thick: gleaming, white, blue, clear, transparent ice. The
5 icecap weighs on the land like a lead brick on a floating plank, pressing it down below the level of the surrounding sea. If the ice were suddenly removed, the waters of the ocean would rush in to its place.

1

It can be reasonably inferred that the people who live in Greenland's coastal towns and villages

A) would welcome a scientific study of icebergs.
B) would strongly consider moving to another location.
C) are exposed to powerful natural forces.
D) are optimistic about their future.

The correct answer is C). According to the passage, *towns and villages cling to the coastline* while enormous glaciers *loom* above them. If for any reason the ice were suddenly removed, the ocean waters would *rush in* and inundate everything in its path. Taken together, this evidence supports the answer that the people who live in Greenland's towns and villages are exposed to *powerful* natural forces. Choices A) and B) may be true but are beyond the scope of this passage. Choice D) is entirely subjective and not supported by the passage.

Practice Paragraph #3

Franklin was named after the great Philadelphia patriot and amateur scientist Benjamin Franklin. But unlike his namesake, our Franklin grew up in a remote corner of eastern Tennessee that seemed like 5 the edge of the world. Like everyone else in his world Franklin's home had a radio and one well-worn Bible. Apart from an occasional person who visited Johnson City, few people ventured outside their small mountain town. Franklin lived in an insulated society 10 that was as yet untouched by another Franklin – President Franklin D. Roosevelt and his New Deal.

1

Which choice best summarizes this paragraph?

A) A central character prepares to face an impending crisis.

B) A central character lives an isolated life in an obscure location.

C) A central character is eager to expand his horizons.

D) A central character is absorbed in his past.

The correct answer is B). The key phrases *remote corner*, *edge of the world*, and *insulated society* all provide evidence that Franklin lives "an isolated life." Answer choice A) is tempting: the passage does conclude by hinting that big changes are coming to eastern Tennessee. However, there is no evidence that these changes will present Franklin with a crisis. Answer choices C) and D) may be true, but they are not supported by the passage.

Evidence-Based Pairs: Introduction

The SAT Reading Test now includes a significant number of new combination questions known as Evidence-Based Pairs. The pair begins with a normal question asking you about an aspect of the passage. It is followed by a question that always asks, *Which choice provides the best evidence for the answer to the previous question?* The four answer choices consist of quotations from the passage, one of which will contain the information necessary to answer the first question.

Each Reading Test passage includes one and usually two sets of Evidence-Based Pairs. Our analysis of these questions indicates that they are in fact a subtle and sophisticated way to test your ability to identify and understand the meaning of selected vocabulary words. These paired questions offer you both rewards and risks. If you understand and recognize the key vocabulary words, you can easily add two points to your raw score. However, if you misunderstand the questions you risk losing both points. Don't worry! We have devised a three-step strategy designed to help you master the Evidence-Based Pairs.

Let's look at an example:

Political scientists have carefully studied the impact of Dr. King's life and speeches on public attitudes towards civil rights. The opening of the Martin Luther King, Jr. Memorial in Washington,
5 D.C., on August 22, 2011 provided an excellent opportunity to continue this investigative tradition. Thousands of people visit the memorial each day to pay tribute to Dr. King and to honor his vision of a just society. After admiring the thirty-foot statue of
10 Dr. King, most visitors stand in front of the Inscription Wall and reverently read the inscribed excerpts from his most inspiring sermons and public addresses. Our team of public opinion experts began their research by interviewing a random selection of
15 visitors to gauge how visiting the memorial affected their view of civil rights in America.

1

The passage indicates that visitors approach Dr. King's words with an attitude of

A) detached indifference.
B) open disapproval.
C) quiet skepticism.
D) great admiration.

2

Which choice provides the best evidence for the answer to the previous question?

A) Lines 1-3 ("Political...rights")
B) Lines 3-6 ("The opening...tradition")
C) Lines 9-13 ("After...addresses")
D) Lines 13-16 ("Our...America")

Step 1: Begin by carefully determining what the first question is asking. The key word *attitude* tells you what to look for in the passage.

Step 2: Next, read each of the four sentences referenced in the answer choices. As you read each choice, look for a key word or phrase that describes the "attitude" of visitors as they approached Dr. King's famous words. The key word *reverently* clearly describes their attitude.

Step 3: Now match the meaning of *reverently* with one of the answer choices in the first question. As you learned in our list of vocabulary words, *reverently* (see Word #34) means "with great admiration." You have a match! The answers to our two questions are D) and C).

Evidence-Based Pairs: Guided Practice

Because they often ask you to consider information from such a large portion of a passage, Evidence-Based Pairs can seem like a daunting challenge. Practicing our three-step approach will build your confidence and produce impressive results. The following three examples are designed to provide you with additional guided practice.

Example #1

The cockroach is roughly 250 million years old, which makes it one of the planet's oldest living insects. As it happens, the cockroach is a particularly popular test subject for laboratory research. It adapts
5   well to captivity, lives relatively long, reproduces quickly, and will subsist in full vigor on Purina Dog Chow. The largest American species, up to two inches in length and known as *Periplaneta Americana*, is even big enough for easy dissection. One eminent
10 physiologist has written fondly: "The laboratory investigator who keeps up a battle to rid his rat colony of cockroaches may well consider giving up the rats and working with the cockroaches instead. From many points of view the roach is practically made to
15 order as a laboratory subject. Here is an animal of frugal habits, tenacious of life, eager to live in the laboratory and every modest in its space requirements."

1

The passage most directly suggests that the cockroach displays impressive behavioral traits that make it a desirable laboratory subject because

A) it has existed since prehistoric times.
B) it is small but clever.
C) it is a defiant creature that resists captivity.
D) it is persistent and determined.

2

Which choice provides the best evidence for the answer to the previous question?

A) Lines 1-3 ("The cockroach…insects")
B) Lines 4-7 ("It adapts…Chow")
C) Lines 7-9 ("The largest…dissection")
D) Lines 15-18 ("Here is…requirements")

Step 1: Begin by carefully determining what the first question is asking. The key phrase *impressive behavior traits* tells you what to look for in the passage.

Step 2: Next, read each of the four sentences referenced in the answer choices. As you read each choice, look for a key word or phrase that describes an "impressive behavioral trait." The key phrase *tenacious of life* is clearly such a trait.

Step 3: Now match the meaning of *tenacious* with one of the answer choices in the first question. As you learned in our list of words, *tenacious* (see Word #32) means "persistent and determined." You have a match! The answers to these two questions are D) and D). Although choice A) is a true statement, it is an incorrect answer because it does not describe a behavioral trait. Choices B) and C) are wrong because the passage indicates that they are factually incorrect.

Example #2

Anthropologist Edward T. Hall contends that cultural differences can be reflected in the ways that people perceive time. In his book, *The Silent Language*, Hall says that these perceptions "speak" as
5 much as words and other symbols; they comprise, in effect, the silent language of culture.

Hall maintains that Americans are a clock-bound people, acutely aware of time. We regard time as a commodity. We say, for example, "Time is money,"
10 and that time can be bought, sold, spent, lost, made up, and measured. We praise entrepreneurs who use time efficiently and scorn those who waste time and thus weaken their chance at success.

Not all cultures are as obsessed with "beating the
15 clock" as our own. What happens when Americans find themselves in a society that has a more relaxed attitude toward time? The result may be culture shock.

1

According to the passage, Americans believe that misusing time can

A) prevent people from learning how to enjoy life.
B) prevent people from learning how to interpret the silent language of culture.
C) undermine a person's chance of achieving success.
D) induce a feeling of cultural shock.

2

Which choice provides the best evidence for the answer to the previous question?

A) Lines 2-3 ("Cultural…time")
B) Lines 3-6 ("In his…culture")
C) Lines 11-13 ("We praise…success")
D) Lines 15-17 ("What happens…shock")

Step 1: Begin by carefully determining what the first question is asking. The key phrase *misusing time* tells us to look for a negative consequences of mishandling time.

Step 2: Next, read each of the four sentences referenced in the answer choices. As you read each choice, look for a key word or phrase that describes the impact of misusing time. The key phrase *weaken their chance of success* clearly identifies a negative impact.

Step 3: Now match the meaning of *weaken* with one of the answer choices in the first sentence. As you learned in our list of key words, *undermine* (see Word #13) means "to damage or weaken." You have a match! The answers to our two questions are C) and C). Choice D) is wrong because it provides an example of a possible consequence of Americans' *more relaxed attitude toward time*. This differs from an impact of *misusing time*. Choices A) and B) are not supported by the passage.

Now let's try something longer.

Example #3

For millennia, humans have probed the nature and purpose of sleep. Aristotle suggested that sleep was restorative, a time to replace or rebuild all that was burned up throughout the body during the day.
5 Modern science supports this idea, with researchers identifying sets of genes associated with restoration and metabolic pathways that turn on only during sleep. Chiara Cirelli and her colleague Giulio Tononi focus on sleep's effect on the brain. In a paper
10 published in 2003, they hypothesized about sleep's role in the growth of synapses, which serve as avenues to ferry information among neurons. Synapses are constantly strengthening, or widening, during the day to accommodate the flow of traffic as
15 the brain soaks up new experiences. But that strengthening cannot go on indefinitely, or else the synapses will become saturated—think "information overload."
    The researchers suggested in their earlier paper
20 that synapses get pruned back during sleep. This pruning doesn't necessarily cause the body to need sleep; rather, the body is taking advantage of the decreased brain traffic that occurs while an individual sleeps. To find evidence for this, the researchers used
25 a new form of electron microscopy that can discern the miniscule changes in the shrinking and subsequent expansion of these microscopic synapses at the nanometer level in mice brains. They found that a few hours of sleep led to an 18 percent decrease in the size
30 of the synapses on average.
    Cirelli said that one interesting finding was that this pruning occurred in about 80 percent of the synapses but spared the largest ones. These larger synapses may be associated with the memories most fundamental to a
35 person's identity, connections the brain does not want to lose, the researchers speculated. Yet, the way in which the brain decides what synaptic connections to prune is another mystery to explore, Cirelli said.

1

Which choice best reflects the perspective of the "researchers" (line 19) on the reduction of synapses during sleep?

A) Even small amounts of sleep lead to a reduction in every type of synapse.
B) Synapses responsible for essential memories are less likely to be eliminated during sleep than are other types of synapses.
C) Sleep occurs as a result of the body's need to reduce the number of synapses.
D) Synapses that are most active during the day experience the greatest reduction during sleep.

2

Which choice provides the best evidence for the answer to the previous question?

A) Lines 15-17 ("But...saturated")
B) Lines 20-22 ("This ...sleep")
C) Lines 28-30 ("They...average")
D) Lines 33-35 ("These...identity")

Step 1: As always, begin with a careful analysis of the question. The key word *perspective* and the key phrase *reduction of synapses during sleep* both tell you what to look for in the passage.

Step 2: Next, read each of the sentences referenced in the answer choices. As you read each choice, look for a key word or phrase that describes the "perspective" of researchers on the reduction of synapses during sleep. The key word *fundamental* clearly describes how the researchers perceive the larger synapses.

Step 3: Now match the meaning of *fundamental* with one of the answer choices in the first question. As you learned in our list of vocabulary words, *fundamental* (see Word #9) means "basic and essential." You have a match! The answers to the two questions are B) and D).

Evidence-Based Pairs: Independent Practice

The following full-length passage will give you an opportunity to apply our three-step process to two sets of Evidence-Based Pairs.

William Foote Whyte's study of an impoverished Italian-American slum he called "Cornerville"—Boston's North End—is a classic of sociological research. Whyte lived and worked in
5 Cornerville during the final years of the Great Depression between 1937 and 1940. He later published his findings in a book titled *Street Corner Society*.

Whyte research relied almost entirely on the
10 method of participant observation. He did not pretend to study Cornerville's major institutions. Indeed, he scarcely mentioned the family, the church, the schools, and the legitimate sectors of the local economy. Instead, Whyte focused on mapping the
15 intricate social worlds of two associations in which he participated, a street corner gang called the Nortons and a small association called the Italian Community Club. The members of the Nortons were "corner boys" whose life revolved around particular street
20 corners and nearby shops. The members of the Italian Community Club were "college boys" who focused on getting a good education so they could move up the social ladder. The social distance between the lives of the two groups was one of the major themes
25 in Whyte's book.

Street Corner Society has a remarkable dramatic quality. Few other works in the sociological literature contain such vivid portrayals of real people in real situations. Much of this quality must be attributed to
30 Whyte's emotional involvement with the people he studied. The clarity of his extensive use of direct quotations provides the reader with a sense of personal involvement.

Whyte grew up in an affluent family that was far
35 removed from Cornerville. He nonetheless performed his task of being a participant observer so well that he did not seem out of place. He found a second home in the family of a local restaurant keeper, learned Italian, achieved high status in the Nortons, made friends with
40 the racketeers, worked in election campaigns, and even brought his new bride to live in Cornerville. Whyte sometimes forgot neutrality and took sides in local issues. For example, on one occasion he voted several times on election day. Critics have
45 complained that Whyte often lost his objectivity and sometimes turned from being a nonparticipating observer to being a nonobserving participant.

The best remembered of Whyte's findings is known as the bowling score effect. Bowling was one of
50 the Norton's principle activities. Sociologists had long held that an individual's skill in a sport would contribute to his or her status in the group. However, after an extensive observation of bowling competition, Whyte hypothesized that the reverse was actually true -
55 the status of a group member determined his or her bowling skill. This was particularly true on those occasions when the entire group assembled for an important match. Subtle and overt group pressures were deliberately used to depress the performance of
60 lower-ranking group members. At the same time, positive group pressures were employed to sustain the performance of the leaders. Whyte vividly reported this phenomenon in one of his most quoted passages:

Here was the social structure in action on the
65 *bowling alleys. It held the individual members in their places—and I along with them. I did not stop to reason then that, as a close friend of Doc, Danny, and Mike, I held a position close to the top of the gang and therefore should be expected to excel on this great*
70 *occasion. I simply felt myself buoyed up by the situation. I felt my friends were for me, had confidence in me, wanted me to bowl well. As my turn came and I stepped up to bowl, I felt supremely confident that I was going to hit the pins that I was aiming at. I have*
75 *never felt quite this way before – or since. Here at the bowling alley I was experiencing subjectively the impact of the group structure upon the individual. It was a strange feeling, as if something larger than myself was controlling the ball as I went through my*
80 *swing and released it toward the pins.*

Although Whyte was not an outstanding bowler, he won the tournament for the Nortons. His insights into the positive and negative effects of group performance have influenced subsequent sociological
85 studies.

1

The author most directly stresses which point about the inequalities of life in Cornerville?

A) The obvious lack of social cohesion.
B) The detrimental effect of a corrupt political system.
C) The disparity between the lives of two principal social groups.
D) The pervasive feeling of pessimism caused by difficult economic conditions.

2

Which choice provides the best evidence for the answer to the previous question?

A) Lines 4-6 ("Whyte lived...1940")
B) Lines 23-25 ("The social ...book")
C) Lines 34-35 ("Whyte grew...Cornerville")
D) Lines 43-44 ("For example...day")

3

According to the passage, the bowling score effect is significant because it

A) called into question an earlier consensus.
B) demonstrated flaws in the participation observation method.
C) provided evidence for a popular viewpoint.
D) illustrated the underlying social antagonisms in Cornerville.

4

Which choice provides the best evidence for the answer to the previous question?

A) Lines 48-49 ("The best...effect")
B) Lines 50-56 ("Sociologists...skill")
C) Lines 56-58 ("This...match")
D) Lines 58-62 ("Subtle...leaders")

Answers: Questions #1 and #2

Step 1: Begin by carefully determining what Question #1 is asking. The key phrase *inequalities of life* tells you what to look for in the passage.

Step 2: Next, read each of the four passage sentences referenced in the answer choices. As you read each answer choice look for a key word or phrase describing the "inequalities of life" in Cornerville. They key phrase *social distance* in line 23 clearly indicates a connection to the idea of inequalities.

Step 3: Now match the phrase *social distance* in line 23 with one of the answer choices in Question #1. As you learned in our list of vocabulary words, *disparity* (see Word #35) means "a condition of inequality." Now you have a match! The answer to Question #1 is therefore C), and the answer to Question #2 is B).

Answers: Questions #3 and #4

Step 1: Begin by carefully determining what Question #3 is asking. The key word *significant* tells you to look for a reason why the bowling score effect is important.

Step 2: Next, read each of the four sentences referenced in the answer choices. As you read each choice, look for a key word or phrase indicating why the bowling score effect is significant. The key phrases *Sociologists had long held* (lines 50-51) and *However after an extensive observation* (lines 52-53) clearly indicate that Whyte made *a significant observation*.

Step 3: Now match the phrases *Sociologists had long held* and *However, after extensive observation* with one of the answer choices in Question #3. As you learned in our list of vocabulary words, *consensus* (see Word #8) means "a general agreement." Whyte's observation is significant because it called into question an earlier consensus. You have a match! The answer to Question #3 is therefore A), and the answer to Question #4 is B).

Answers: Matching Set #1

1. B

Insufficient = weak, support = evidence

2. D

This question requires you to understand how authors can imply a position rather than state it outright. To say that something *had long been thought* is to imply that it is a broadly accepted explanation—that is, it is the product of a *consensus* (general agreement). SAT passages, however, are more concerned with *new* theories—ones that threaten to overturn an accepted explanation. Statements such as *it had long been thought* thus signal that the author is discussing a theory that has been *questioned* or discredited.

3. E

Hopeful = optimistic, future = going forward

4. C

To say that something is based on *extensive speculation* is to say that it is based on a lot of guesswork. In other words, it has not been conclusively proven based on factual (i.e. empirical) data or observation.

5. A

Random = haphazard

Answers: Matching Set #2

1. E

Tentative means "uncertain" or "subject to change," so something tentative is *still unsettled.*

2. D

Retard = slow down, and commerce = economic activity. If commerce is "retarded," economic success (i.e. *prosperity*) is endangered.

3. A

A trait that is *attributable to genetics* is by definition an inborn trait, i.e. *necessarily innate.*

4. C

Immense = great, distance = disparities. Note that *great* is used in a second meaning here. Likewise, *distance* does not denote the space between two objects; rather, it indicates two non-equivalent things.

5. B

Enlarge = open, minds = thoughts

Part II: Writing

Chapter 3: Commonly Confused Words

....

"The difference between the almost right word and the right word is really a large matter. 'tis the difference between the lightning bug and the lightning."

-Mark Twain

There's no question that English can be very tricky sometimes. It's filled with **homophones**—words that have slightly different spellings but that are pronounced similarly or identically. When people speak quickly, as is often the case in everyday conversation, these words can be impossible to tell apart. But while errors can easily be hidden in speech, they are far more obvious in writing.

For example, take a look at the following paragraph:

> Before the first transatlantic cables were manufactured, communication between North America and Europe was limited. Accept for ships, which took weeks to cross the ocean, there was no way to relay messages between continents. Making matters worse, severe winter storms could have an averse affect on correspondence, delaying ships for weeks and depriving individuals and companies of excess to family members and business associates. Five attempts to lay a cable were made between 1857 and 1866, but workers were unable to make all of the pieces cohere to the bottom of the ocean; there was always apart that broke away. In 1866, however, a lasting connection was finally achieved. The new cable immediately effected communication times, assuring that people could send a message and receive a response the same day.

Did you notice anything odd as you read this paragraph? It includes a number of commonly confused words tested on recent (P)SATs. Don't worry if you looked past them—that's the point!

Now take a look at the corrected version:

> Before the first transatlantic cables were manufactured, communication between North America and Europe was limited. **Except** for ships, which took weeks to cross the ocean, there was no way to relay messages between continents. Making matters worse, severe winter storms could have an **adverse effect** on correspondence, delaying ships for weeks and depriving individuals and companies of **access** to family members and business associates. Five attempts to lay a cable were made between 1857 and 1866, but workers were unable to make all of the pieces **adhere** to the bottom of the ocean; there was always **a part** that broke away. In 1866, however, a lasting connection was finally achieved. The new cable immediately **affected** communication times, **ensuring** that people could send a message and receive a response in same day.

The good news is that you'll never see anything like this example on the (P)SAT. You will encounter no more than two questions testing this concept on the Writing test. More good news: the SAT often tests the same **limited group** of homophones over and over again. If you want to be prepared and not risk losing easy points, however, you must be familiar with the top contenders for this error.

Affect vs. Effect

Of all the word pairs tested on the SAT, **affect vs. effect** tends to give students the most trouble. So naturally College Board test writers devote a number of questions to this troublesome pair of words. But don't worry! This section will help you ace affect vs. effect questions.

Affect is a verb meaning "to influence or have an impact on something." For example, the forecast for a big winter storm **affected** the plans of people throughout the entire metropolitan area.

Effect is usually a noun* meaning "the result or consequence of something." If *a/an/the* appears before the word, the answer is *effect*. *Effect* is often followed by *on* because things have "an effect on" other things. For example, the Boston Tea Party had an immediate **effect on** relations between the colonies and Great Britain; it was **effective** (adjective form of *effect*) in getting the King's attention.

Although these words can be very confusing, you can also use the following mnemonic trick to help you keep them straight. Think **RAVEN**: **R**emember **A**ffect is a **V**erb and **E**ffect is a **N**oun.

Guided Practice:

Example #1

Incorrect:	The accumulation of oxygen in the atmosphere **effects** the amount of sunlight that reaches the ground.
Correct:	The accumulation of oxygen in the atmosphere **affects** the amount of sunlight that reaches the ground.

The subject of this sentence is *the accumulation of oxygen*. Note that *affect* is a verb since *the accumulation of oxygen…affects*.

Example #2

Incorrect:	The accumulation of oxygen in the atmosphere has **an affect on** the amount of sunlight that reaches the ground.
Correct:	The accumulation of oxygen in the atmosphere has **an effect on** the amount of sunlight that reaches the ground.

Effect is correct because *an* must come before a noun, and the word in question is followed by *on*.

Example #3

Classical computers encode information as bits that can be in one of two states: zero or one. In contrast, quantum computers are composed of "qubits" that can be in both states simultaneously. These qubits have the **[effect/affect]** of allowing computers to essentially perform many calculations at once.

Because *the* appears before the word, a noun is required. *Effect* is therefore the only possible answer.

*__Note:__ There are situations in which *affect* is used as a noun and *effect* as a verb; however, the College Board appears to be uninterested in testing these exceptions, and they should not concern you here.

Independent Practice #1: Affect vs. Effect
(Answers p. 75)

1. The Luck Knot Bridge in Changsha, China, twists and folds in a seemingly never-ending loop. The designers of the bridge knew that the structure had to hang at least 78 feet above the river, and that in order to accommodate pedestrians, its sharpest incline could not exceed 34 degrees. The **[affect/effect]** of these constraints was to produce a structure that resembles a roller coaster.

2. As cell phones have proliferated, drivers have increasingly begun talking and texting while behind the wheel. Unsurprisingly, accident rates have risen, and now, states are taking steps to restrict cell phone use among drivers. In Oregon, New York, and Maryland, for example, laws that prohibit drivers from holding phones while operating vehicles have gone into **[affect/effect]**.

3. Each year, a program run jointly by the California Avocado Commission and the University of California-Riverside plants three new varieties of avocado at various locations in the heart of avocado territory. The goal is to study how the environment **[affects/effects]** the plants' growth, and to keep watch for outliers that perform well in extreme temperatures.

4. On their treks to the South Pole, Shackleton, Scott, and Amundsen faced hardships from frostbite to snow blindness. Much of their misery, however, was caused by the ideal gas law, which describes how pressure **[affects/effects]** the volume and temperature of a gas. It is this law that explains why the Antarctic surface is buffeted by winds of up to 200 miles per hour.

5. Light comes in two different forms. There is visible light, which can be seen from a long way away. Then there is invisible light, which comes in the form of radio signals, internet signals, and mobile phone signals. This light makes a web of electromagnetic waves that we walk through. Although it cannot be seen directly, it **[affects/effects]** our use of radios, television, and the internet.

6. As the smallest birds on earth, hummingbirds may seem frail, but in reality they are actually quite hardy. When the temperature drops, these birds enter into a state known as "torpor," which has the **[affect/effect]** of helping them conserve energy. Birds that remain north during the winter experience a nightly "mini-hibernation" in which their 107-degree body temperatures can plummet to 48 degrees. The cold also **[affects/effects]** the birds' heart rates, which slow from over 1,200 beats per minute to 50 to 180 beats.

7. A new type of remote control uses sensors to determine the remote's exact location. As a result, when the device is pointed at a lamp or a television, it "knows" exactly what it's looking at. This contextual awareness **[affects/effects]** the user's experience by making the fragmented experience of the smart home feel simpler and more intuitive.

8. The slip of tectonic plates and the fiery eruptions of volcanoes reflect the constantly shifting conditions below the Earth's surface. Our planet is composed of layers, each of which plays a different role in protecting life from the solar storms and moderating the climate. Although it remains hidden from our daily view, the ground below our feet is a dynamic environment that **[affects/effects]** us every day.

9. The impact of the Chicxulub asteroid, which wiped out large dinosaurs and giant marine reptiles, had a global **[affect/effect]**: it created a layer of debris that spread across every continent and that is now part of the geologic record. Geologists refer to this layer as the Cretaceous–Paleogene boundary because it marks the switch between these two geologic time periods.

10. In 1776, Thomas Paine published *Common Sense*, the pamphlet in which he made public a persuasive and impassioned case for the American Colonies' independence from Great Britain. Its **[affect/effect]** was instantaneous: previously, full independence had not been considered a real possibility, but Paine's writing convinced the colonists that it should be given serious consideration.

Additional Commonly Confused Words to Know

A part is two words, and refers a portion or section of something, e.g. a pizza or a pie. **Apart** is one word meaning "separate" or "with the exception of." For example, you could say that **apart** from the SAT and two AP exams, you are finished with standardized testing. You could also say that **apart** from being on the soccer team, you're not spending a lot of time on sports this semester.

Access can be either a verb meaning "to be able to enter" or a noun meaning "the ability or right to enter." For example, you could steal your brother's password in order to **access** (verb) his computer, or to gain **access** (noun) to it. **Excess**, on the other hand, can be either a noun or an adjective meaning "more than the required amount." If you have an **excess** of time, or an **excess** amount of time on your hands, you might decide to try to find the password to your brother's computer.

Accept is a verb meaning "receive," e.g. "Although I was less than thrilled with the pair of ugly socks my aunt gave me for my birthday, I manage to **accept** them with a smile." **Except** means "excluding." If you were writing thank-you notes for those birthday gifts, you might be tempted to send one to everyone **except** your aunt.

Adhere means "stick to." If you've ever put on an **adhesive** bandage (i.e. a Band Aid™) after cutting yourself, that's where the term comes from. Likewise, if you've ever stepped on a piece of gum, you might have had some trouble getting it off because it was **adhering** so strongly to the sole of your shoe. On the other hand, the somewhat similar verb **cohere** means "hold together." For example, your English teacher might give you a poor grade on the essay you wrote about *The Great Gatsby* at 2 a.m. on the day it was due because your argument didn't **cohere**—that is, you introduced points randomly and never really explained how they fit together.

Adverse means "negative" or "unpleasant." For example, if someone is allergic to peanuts, exposure to even a small amount of that food can produce an **adverse** reaction such as hives, dizziness, or even shock. As a result, it's no wonder that people with peanut allergies tend to be strongly **averse** to (inclined to avoid) situations in which they might be accidentally exposed to peanuts. Some people who are exceptionally sensitive may even try to avoid being in the same room with them.

To **persecute** is to mistreat someone on the grounds of race, religion, or political belief. For example, Nelson Mandela was **persecuted** for his struggle against apartheid in South Africa: he was harassed and ultimately jailed for many years. To **prosecute** is to implement legal proceedings against someone for a crime. A person caught breaking into a house, for instance, will be **prosecuted**—that is, put on trial and then sent to jail.

To **undertake** is to embark on or to attempt something challenging. For example, a highly motivated student might **undertake** the challenge of juggling multiple AP classes as a sophomore. To **overtake** means "to surpass." For example, a person who is used to always being taller than a younger brother or sister might be surprised when that younger sibling **overtakes** him or her in height. To **take in** can mean "to absorb" (information). For example, if you try to read an entire 300-page book the night before a big test on it, you might have trouble **taking everything in**. This verb can also mean "to be fooled or tricked." For example, senior citizens are often targeted by con artists because they are perceived to be naïve and thus more easily **taken in** than younger people are.

Than is used to form comparisons. For example, you could say that two years ago, your younger brother was three inches shorter **than** you, but now he is three inches taller. In contrast, **then** is a synonym for "next" and is used to indicate sequences of events. For example, you could say that last Friday you went to the movies, and **then** you went out for pizza.

Independent Practice #2: Affect vs. Effect & Additional Pairs
(Answers p. 75)

1. Passage of the Perkins Vocational and Technical Act, which provides more than a billion dollars for career and technical education, will help **[assure/ensure]** that essential career and technical education programs equip graduates for current and future high-growth jobs.

2. Large-scale battery storage is likely to undergo unprecedented growth in the United States over the next several years. By 2021, up to 1,800 megawatts of new energy storage are expected to become available. That's eight times more than total U.S. installed energy storage capacity in 2016, and it should translate into nearly 5,900 megawatt-hours of **[access/excess]** power that energy workers can quickly dispatch to address power outages, reduce peak demand charges, or simply improve reliability.

3. To develop a science of refrigerated shipping, Barbara Pratt spent nearly seven years during the 1970s working and living in a refrigerated shipping container that included bunk beds, a microwave, a refrigerator, a shower, and, most importantly, a fully equipped science lab. In addition to monitoring temperature, Pratt mapped the **[affects/effects]** of airflow and humidity on various types of foods.

4. Palmyra Atoll, a refuge for seabird breeding colonies and coral reef communities, is **[a part/apart]** of the Pacific Remote Islands Marine National Monument. Located south of the Hawaiian Islands, the atoll lies nearly 3,500 miles from the nearest continent. Although it contains temporary accommodations for the scientists who come to do research, the atoll has no permanent residents.

5. Harry Houdini is most often remembered as an escape artist and a magician, but he was also an actor, a pilot, a historian, and a businessman. In each of these roles, he was an innovator and sometimes an inventor. He was, however, largely **[adverse/averse to]** taking any action that could reveal the secrets behind his illusions. As a result, he avoided the patent process and generally sought to conceal his inventive nature.

6. At the office, healthcare workers know how to diagnose and treat their patients. They even know what treatment plans to provide. They cannot, however, control what patients do when they are on their own. According to researchers, patients with chronic conditions **[adhere/cohere to]** their care plan only 50% of the time. This is especially dangerous because willingness to abide by recommendations about medication and lifestyle changes can determine a patient's fate.

7. Al Capone's seven-year reign as a crime boss ended when he was 33 years old. Federal authorities were intent on jailing Capone, and in 1931 they **[persecuted/prosecuted]** him for tax evasion, which was then a federal crime. During the highly publicized case, the judge admitted as evidence Capone's admissions of his income and unpaid taxes during prior negotiations.

8. At the age of six, Frederick Douglass began his life as a slave. By the standards of his time, Douglass often received favored treatment, but his daily life also included hunger, cold, and savage beatings. These realities of slavery were an outrage that Douglass refused to **[accept/except]** almost from the first day, and they inspired him to begin a struggle that would both anger and inspire millions of people.

9. Modern scientific equipment can be staggeringly difficult to obtain. For example, take the NanoSIMS probe, an instrument that picks apart a few atoms at a time. Only 22 exist in the entire world. Even widely used scientific equipment is expensive and requires significant expertise to run. At the Princeton Plasma Physics Laboratory, however, the goal is to give high school students **[access/excess to]** sophisticated equipment by letting them work remotely.

10. Emanuele Fornasier, a photographer and chemist, has filmed a high-speed version of electrocrystallization, a process whereby a metal in liquid solution forms crystals after being exposed to an electric current. Fornasier wanted to create crystals growing in a dendritic structure, and he **[undertook/overtook]** a project that would allow him to capture them on film. To achieve the correct **[affect/effect]**, he created solutions with a high concentration of metal ions. He then let the crystals grow overnight, while a very low current ran through the solution.

Glossary of Commonly Confused Words

Afflict – v., cause pain; used to emphasize that someone is suffering. Although it is correct to say that x afflicts someone, it is more common to say that someone is afflicted *with* x.
Ex: Because she has been **afflicted** with the condition since she was very young, she has learned to manage it well.

Inflict – v., force pain or suffering upon someone. Used to emphasize that someone or something is causing pain. X is inflicted (up)on someone.
Ex: Last night at dinner, my aunt **inflicted** photos of her vacation to Poughkeepsie on me and my brother.

Allude – refer to
Ex: My friend **alluded** to the movie during our conversation, but because I had not seen it, I did not understand the reference.

Elude – avoid, evade
Ex: By living in the woods and foraging for food, the escaped convict successfully **eluded** capture for almost a month.

Ambivalent – having mixed feelings
Ex: I am **ambivalent** about having a younger brother: on one hand, it's nice to have someone look up to me, but on the other hand, he can be very annoying.

Ambiguous – unclear, able to be interpreted multiple ways
Ex: The directions for the paper were **ambiguous**: it wasn't clear whether we needed to have the teacher approve our sources before we started writing, or whether we could submit them later.

Anecdote – brief story
Ex: History is my favorite class because my teacher always tells amusing **anecdotes** about famous historical figures.

Antidote – substance that counteracts a poison
Ex: Because it has no known **antidote**, pufferfish toxin is one of the most dangerous substances on earth.

Appraise – evaluate, assess the value of
Ex: After the house was gut-renovated and modernized, it was **appraised** at nearly twice its original value.

Apprise – inform
Ex: Bound by disclosure regulations, the real estate agent **apprised** the potential buyers of a number of structural problems with the house.

Censor – Remove offensive or inappropriate parts
Ex: In pre-Revolutionary France, royal **censors** exercised great power over which books could be distributed to the public.

Censure – Punish
Ex: After it was reported that the senator had used campaign funds for his personal expenses, he was **censured** by his colleagues.

Collaborate – work with
Ex: Because Leila and I had never gotten along well, I was none too thrilled when the teacher asked us to **collaborate** on the project.

Corroborate – confirm, make certain
Ex: After trying in vain to contact the source for several weeks, the reporter was finally able to **corroborate** the story.

Descent – n., going down
Ex: Our **descent** into the cave was made more difficult by the numerous rocks lining the ground.

Dissent – n., v., go against popular opinion
Ex: Almost the entire class was unanimous in wanting the test postponed until after vacation; only one student **dissented** and asked that it be given before.

Disinterested – objective
Ex: It is crucial that judges be entirely **disinterested** in the cases over which they preside: any form of bias would make a fair trial impossible.

Uninterested – not interested
Ex: The child appeared thoroughly uninterested in the toy; he showed no inclination to play or engage with it in any way.

Elicit – draw out
Ex: Because the teacher's question seemed so ridiculous, it **elicited** a number of laughs.

Illicit – illegal, not permitted
Ex: Although they attempted to hide their presence, the trespassers were arrested for **illicit** activity.

Eminent – important, renowned (person)
Ex: Because the person accused of the crime was an **eminent** physician, no one could believe that he was guilty.

Imminent – about to occur
Ex: In regions with heavy volcanic activity, earthquakes often signal that an eruption is **imminent**.

Exhaustive – thorough
Ex: The search was **exhaustive**, covering nearly 100 miles and lasting five weeks, but no one could find any trace of the missing hikers.

Exhausting – tiring
Ex: The calculus final lasted two hours and was so **exhausting** that I fell asleep as soon as I arrived home.

Formally – (1) officially; (2) in a refined manner

Ex (1): The council voted to adopt the resolution but agreed to delay **formally** implementing it for six months.

Ex (2): My grandmother is a very elegant woman: she behaves more **formally** than anyone I know.

Formerly – in the past

Ex: The largest city in Turkey is now called Istanbul, but it was **formerly** known as Constantinople.

Implicit – implied, not directly stated

Ex: The threat was **implicit** from the look on his face; he did not need to say a word to make his anger apparent.

Complicit – responsible for participating in something bad or illegal

Ex: At the trial, the defendant insisted that he was not at all **complicit** in the crime—that he had played no role in it and was present at the crime scene only by chance.

Ingenious – clever

Ex: Although I was unable to find a solution to the problem, my friend came up with an **ingenious** approach—one that was both simple and easy to implement.

Ingenuous: naïve

Ex: Senior citizens are common targets for con artists because they are perceived as trusting and **ingenuous**.

Lay – set something down; followed by a noun

Ex: Before going to sleep, I usually **lay** my phone on the table beside my bed.

Lie – stretch out, e.g. to lie down; not followed by a noun

Ex: After hiking for nearly five hours, I was relieved to be able to **lie** down.

Precede – come before

Ex: The beginning of the assembly was **preceded** by a long list of announcements.

Proceed – to go forward, carry on

Ex: After insisting that he would not raise taxes if elected, the politician **proceeded** to do just the opposite.

Use to – does not exist

Used to – (1) accustomed to; (2) indicates a frequently performed action in the past

Ex (1): I'm **used to** waking up at 6 a.m. to get to school on time, so this year I was thrilled to discover my first class didn't begin until 8:30.

Ex (2): I **used to** wake up early to play soccer every Saturday morning, but recently I've been sleeping late on weekends.

Wrong Connotation

A second type of wrong-word question involves words that have similar literal meanings but that are used in different contexts.

In addition, these questions test **register**—that is, how formal or informal a word is. The vast majority of the passages that appear on the SAT Writing test are written in a moderately serious, straightforward style. They are not overly literary or casual, but somewhere in between. Essentially, they are intended to approximate the type of writing that will be expected of you in college.

As a result, words that are too formal or informal are unlikely to be correct. Note that incorrect answers are more likely to contain words that are too casual (e.g. *stuff*) than ones that are too formal.

Unfortunately, there is no way to predict which words might be tested on a given exam. The best way to prepare is to read and familiarize yourself with how a variety of common terms are used.

If you get stuck, however, you might find it helpful to plug in your own (simple) word and then search for the best match among the answer choices. Sometimes—though not always—the differences in meaning between the answers will be just big enough for this strategy to be effective.

Guided Practice

1.   As more shops and transport networks adapt to swipe-based cards and touch-and-go mobile technology, many major cities around the world are in the process of knocking off cash to second-class status. Shops, cafes, and buses in some large urban areas are have begun refusing to handle notes or coins.

1

A) NO CHANGE
B) relegating
C) insulting
D) expelling

Devaluing, relegating, insulting, and *expelling* are all negative words that imply criticizing or refuting the importance of something, but they all have different connotations.

Knocking off can either refer to pushing something to the ground from a higher position (e.g. *The boy walked into the statue and knocked it off its pedestal*); or, more colloquially, it can mean producing a cheap imitation of an expensive good (e.g. *The label on the handbag said Louis Vuitton, but it had clearly been knocked off*). However, this word cannot be used to describe cash's reduction in status. It does not have quite the right connotation, and it is also **too informal**.

Relegating means "sending to an inferior position," which fits with the idea that in some places cash is now perceived as having *second class-status*. This word is therefore an exact match.

Insulting is something that is typically done to a person. In addition, the passage does not indicate that people are saying bad things about cash, but rather that consumers and stores/public transportation are considering it outdated. So this word does not fit either.

Expelling means "kicking out," but it is typically used in school-related context. A student can be expelled from school, but cash cannot be "expelled" to a lower status. D) is wrong as well.

B) is the best match, so it is correct.

Let's look at another example.

2. With camera in hand, botanist Ed Croom has been photographing Rowan Oak for more than a decade. He often visits the Oxford, Mississippi, property where William Faulkner wrote his novels, just before the sun rises. At that time, the landscape is still **2** cloaked in mist, and the crowds of tourists have not yet begun to trickle in for tours of the property.

2

A) NO CHANGE
B) bound
C) stashed
D) constrained

If you wanted to plug in your own word here, you might say something like *covered*. Based on the context, that seems like the most logical definition.

Then, consider the answers.

If you're not sure you like how **cloaked** sounds, leave it. It's a synonym for *covered*, so consider it a possibility.

Bound means "tied up," and it has a distinctly negative connotation. In contrast, the passage is describing a peaceful morning scene. So no, this word does not make sense.

Stashed is a little on the casual side. For example, you might stash candy under your bed. It doesn't really fit with the image of mist and mountains. C) can thus be eliminated as well.

Constrained means "limited," which doesn't make a lot of sense either. If you don't know what this word means, think of it this way: the new SAT is designed to focus on "relevant" words, so provided that you have a solid vocabulary, you should generally know the definitions of correct answers. Conversely, if you don't know the definition of a word, it's probably **too formal** and therefore incorrect.

So by process of elimination, we've determined that the answer is A).

On the next page, try a few on your own.

Independent Practice #3: Wrong Connotation

1.   On January 14, 2005, the Huygens probe became the first robotic explorer to touch down on the hazy orange surface of Saturn's moon Titan. During the hour before its batteries died, the probe frantically **1** stacked up data and took detailed pictures to send back to scientists on Earth. During its descent and brief time on the surface, the probe amassed enough data to give scientists a glimpse of an alien world that looks deceptively like Earth.

1

A) NO CHANGE
B) gathered
C) hoarded
D) convened

2.   Grapefruits are a recent discovery, less than 300 years old, but citrus fruit is ancient. Fossilized leaves discovered in China's Yunnan Province in 2009 and 2011 suggest that these fruits have existed for around seven million years. Today, humans consume only a fraction of the varieties in existence. Out of thousands of types of wild fruit, no more than a few dozen have **2** attained commercial success.

2

A) NO CHANGE
B) racked up
C) snagged
D) actualized

3.   Introspection isn't reserved for ancient Greek philosophers or moody teenagers dressed in black. On the contrary, people are constantly examining their own thoughts, memories, and abilities. These "confidence judgments" help us **3** engage what we need to do. For instance, most people would pull out their GPS or consult an online map to avoid getting lost. Likewise, they would probably return home to double-check the stove if they couldn't remember whether it had been turned off.

3

A) NO CHANGE
B) portray
C) check out
D) assess

Now, try all of the question types combined.

Independent Practice, All Question Types: Set #1

1. The term "varietal honey" refers to the honey gathered from a single type of blossom. Every type of nectar has its own flavor and sugar composition, which depends on the flower that produces it. As a result, the honey reflects the unique taste of the bloom. In 1999, the Savannah Bee Company was **1** founded on that principal. Today, the business produces nearly a dozen varieties of honey, each of which reflects its unique origin.

1
A) NO CHANGE
B) founded on that principle.
C) finding on that principle.
D) found on that principal.

2. For 52 consecutive weeks, the designers Giorgia Lupi and Stefanie Posavec sent illustrations to one another. The two women had made a pact: to create one hand-drawn data visualization per week. The drawings might represent how many animals one designer saw in a given seven-day period, or every time one designer felt a **1** surge of envy. These colorful, curious postcards now fill the pages of *Dear Data*, the permanent record of their project.

1
A) NO CHANGE
B) heap
C) stack
D) accretion

3. When people write about music, they often borrow from the realms of the other senses. High passages are said to "soar," and sad music is described as "blue." For people with synesthesia, however, these words are not just metaphors. These individuals experience a "crossing over" of the senses: the sound of a particular note may **1** illicit visions of purple of orange. Alternately, certain tastes may be associated with particular shapes or colors.

1
A) NO CHANGE
B) elicit
C) extract
D) compress

4. The discovery of penicillin, the first antibiotic, was among the most famous accidents in medical history. In fact, when the British scientist Alexander Fleming arrived in his laboratory one morning in September of 1928, he had no idea that he was about to make a discovery that would **1** have a permanent affect on the course of medical history.

1

A) NO CHANGE
B) be permanently affective to
C) permanently affect
D) permanently effect

5. When the digital currency bitcoin was first introduced, people predicted that it would soon replace the dollar. However, the same things that made the technology attractive also made it impractical. For one thing, it required a type of unreliable and hard-to-use software called a wallet. Bitcoins were also difficult to **1** attain and spend. There were few distributors, and only a small number of merchants **2** accepted them—the currency was just too new.

1

A) NO CHANGE
B) retain
C) obtain
D) contain

2

A) NO CHANGE
B) excepted them
C) excepting for
D) expecting them

6. The challenge of protecting yourself online can feel so overwhelming that it can be tempting to give up on security altogether. There's no question that preventing unauthorized users from gaining **1** access of your data is something of a hassle. However, simple steps such as setting up a password manager and making backups of your files can go **2** along way toward ensuring that your confidential information remains safe.

1

A) NO CHANGE
B) access to
C) excess of
D) excess with

2

A) NO CHANGE
B) along way toward
C) a long way toward
D) a long way

7. Tove Jansson is known around the world as the creator of the Moomins: round white children's book characters that resemble hippopotamuses. However, Jansson has always considered herself a painter, and she finds it frustrating that this side of her work has traditionally been **1** omitted. Jansson grew up in an environment where art and life were intertwined: her father was **2** an imminent sculptor and her mother a graphic artist. By the time she entered her teens, her work had already appeared in magazines, and at art school she was considered a promising student.

1
A) NO CHANGE
B) undone.
C) overlooked.
D) deleted.

2
A) NO CHANGE
B) an eminent
C) a big-time
D) a conspicuous

8. The Mayo Clinic is one of the largest and most prestigious research and treatment facilities in the United States. Its logo, which contains three shields, represents the institution's three-part focus. First and most important is the **1** care of patience, as represented by the central shield. Employees of the clinic are expected to **2** cohere with that principle in every aspect of their work. The other two shields represent education and research, two areas in which the Mayo Clinic has slowly become more prominent.

1
A) NO CHANGE
B) care for patience,
C) caring of patience,
D) care of patients,

2
A) NO CHANGE
B) cohere to that principal
C) adhere to that principle
D) adhere with that principal

9. In the next few decades, companies that invest in workers will **1** proceed to transform their industries in terms of productivity and services. For example, consider manufacturers transitioning to the production of electric vehicles. While an internal combustion engine has thousands of parts, an electric engine contains only a few dozen, each requiring a different set of engineering skills. Companies that must meet national quotas for electric vehicles are retraining their engineers and helping them **2** corroborate the production of those parts.

1
A) NO CHANGE
B) proceed in the transformation
C) precede to transform
D) precede with transforming

2
A) NO CHANGE
B) corroborate in producing
C) collaborate the production
D) collaborate to produce

10. In 2011, IBM in partnership with the New York City Department of Education, launched the Pathways in Technology Early College High School, known as P-Tech. The program blends the traditional four-year high school experience with two years of college. Along the way, IBM provides mentors and internships; the company also gives preference for full-time jobs to P-tech graduates and offers workplace tours **1** to prospective interns.

P-Tech students take college courses as soon as they demonstrate they are ready. Because employers help shape the curriculum, graduates are thought to have a better chance of landing a job **2** then graduates of traditional high school programs do. And because of the advantages it provides, the program could ultimately have a significant **3** effect on problems such as high youth unemployment and low community college completion rates.

1

A) NO CHANGE
B) by prospective
C) for perspective
D) with perceptive

2

A) NO CHANGE
B) than
C) as
D) that

3

A) NO CHANGE
B) affect to
C) affect on
D) affection for

Independent Practice, All Question Types: Set #2

1.   Dark energy, the force responsible for the accelerating expansion of the universe, is still a mystery to scientists— but it is a very important mystery. It turns out that dark energy and dark matter make up roughly 68% and 27% percent of the universe **1** respectably. The rest— everything on Earth, every planet, star, and celestial object ever observed—adds up to less than 5%.

1
A) NO CHANGE
B) respectfully.
C) respectively.
D) effectively.

2.   Vint Cerf, who has spent the last four decades shaping the Internet's development, is joining with a new generation of hackers, archivists, and activists to radically reinvent core technologies that underpin the web. Their goal is to make information on the web more secure and less **1** vulnerable to being censored. In addition, they are attempting to make it easier to preserve.

1
A) NO CHANGE
B) vulnerable to be censured.
C) vulnerable to censure.
D) vulnerable to being censored.

3.   From a "kit" of pigeons to a "muster" of peacocks, words that describe groups of birds can be wonderfully evocative. For example, a "parliament" of owls might **1** aspire a person to think of wise old birds crowding into a government building. Likewise, a "paddling" of ducks cannot help but evoke a flock of bright-yellow birds bobbing gently on the water.

1
A) NO CHANGE
B) aspire a person's thinking
C) inspire a thinking person
D) inspire a person to think

4. Begun in Sweden, the Hoffice movement invites workers—freelancers, entrepreneurs, or full-time employees who can do their jobs remotely—to work at each other's homes in order to **1** uphold productivity and reduce social isolation. Those attending pop-up Hoffice events, which are advertised online, are typically asked to work silently in blocks of around 45 minutes. In between, the group takes breaks together to exercise, meditate, or simply share **2** antidotes over a cup of coffee.

1

A) NO CHANGE
B) bolster
C) rev up
D) reform

2

A) NO CHANGE
B) antidotes with
C) anecdotes over
D) anecdotes with

5. From time it was founded, the *Chicago Tribune* was an active participant in the life of Chicago as well as a standard-bearer for innovative journalism. During the paper's formative years, the *Tribune* was a leading anti-slavery newspaper; it also played **1** apart in the election of President Lincoln. In 1881, the *Tribune* played a key role in reinvigorating the city after the Great Chicago Fire, helping to **2** lure business to the rebuilt city.

1

A) NO CHANGE
B) apart from
C) a part in
D) a part

2

A) NO CHANGE
B) chase
C) trap
D) snare

6. Machine learning is the process by which software developers train an AI (Artificial Intelligence) algorithm, using massive amounts of data relevant to the task at hand. Eventually the algorithm "learns" to **1** cohere to the patterns in the initially provided data, enabling it to recognize similar patterns in unfamiliar data. In the past decade, machine learning has produced speech recognition software, **2** effective web searches, and self-driving cars. It is so pervasive that you probably use it dozens of times a day without knowing it.

1

A) NO CHANGE
B) cohere with
C) adhere to
D) cling to

2

A) NO CHANGE
B) affective
C) affectionate
D) infectious

7. In a few years, people could be eating the next generation of genetically altered foods—potatoes that never turn brown or soybeans that contain a healthier mix of fatty acids. There might also be no indication that something is different about these foods. Although a law could soon require genetically modified ingredients to be **1** disclosed on labels, this new type of gene editing falls outside of current regulations. As a result, foods grown with the help of this technology will likely **2** allude the detection of consumers.

1

A) NO CHANGE
B) imported
C) blabbed about
D) uncovered

2

A) NO CHANGE
B) elude
C) confound
D) run away from

8. The Cinderella story told by Disney is a variation on a common theme: a heroine is **1** prosecuted by an envious stepmother, who ridicules her and treats her like as servant, but she eventually escapes to marry a prince. There are many versions of the Cinderella story, though. Some versions leave out the fairy Godmother; instead, magical plants or talking animals are **2** implicit in the heroine's escape. Another detail that changes is what Cinderella has on her feet. In the Disney version, she's wearing glass slippers, but out of nearly 350 versions of the story, a glass slipper appears in only six.

1

A) NO CHANGE
B) prosecuted as
C) persecuted by
D) persecuted for

2

A) NO CHANGE
B) complicit in
C) complied with
D) complicated by

9. Pedal-assisted electric bikes, or e-bikes, have gained popularity over the last decade, rising steadily to account for 12% of bicycle sales worldwide. However, one group has remained **1** ambiguous about the bikes: cycling enthusiasts. Although they enjoy the higher speeds these bikes offer, they also find that pedal-assisted riding does not fully capture the true bicycling experience. In addition, many serious cyclists are **2** use to lightweight frames and consider the vehicles too clunky.

1

A) NO CHANGE
B) ambivalent
C) hazy
D) vague

2

A) NO CHANGE
B) used as
C) used to
D) using to

10. Science fiction movies often feature "memory chips:" tiny electronic devices that are **1** supplanted by the brain and that allow people to recall every moment of their lives in perfect detail. Now, life is imitating art. Theodore Berger, a biomedical engineer at the University of Southern California, is developing a so-called memory "prosthesis." The device, which is surgically placed directly into the brain, mimics the function of a structure called the hippocampus by electrically **2** stimulating the brain to form memories—at least in rats and monkeys. Eventually, the technology could help individuals **3** inflicted on memory problems, such as stroke and accident victims.

1

A) NO CHANGE
B) implemented with
C) implanted by
D) implanted in

2

A) NO CHANGE
B) simulating the brain in forming
C) simulating the brain to form
D) emulating the brain to form

3

A) NO CHANGE
B) inflicted by
C) afflicted with
D) conflicted with

Answers: Commonly Confused Words Exercises

Independent Practice #1: Affect/Effect

1. effect: the word follows *the*, so the noun *effect* is required.

2. effect: *go into effect* is a fixed phrase.

3. affects: the word is a verb whose subject is *the environment*, so *affects* must be used.

4. affects: the word is a verb whose subject is *pressure*, so *affects* must be used.

5. affects: the word is a verb whose subject is *it*, so *affects* must be used.

6. effect…affects: the first word follows *the*, so the noun *effect* is required; the second word is a verb whose subject is *the cold*, so *affects* must be used.

7. affects: the word is a verb whose subject is *awareness*, so *affects* must be used.

8. affects: the word is a verb whose subject is *environment*, so *affects* must be used.

9. effect: the word is preceded by *a*, so *effect* must be used. It is also preceded by the adjective *global*, and an adjective can only modify a noun.

10. effect: *its* is possessive and can only be followed by a noun, so *effect* must be used.

Independent Practice #2: Affect/Effect + Additional Words

1. Ensure: The word must mean something like "guarantee," a definition that only *ensure* fills. In addition, *ensure* is followed by *that*, whereas *assure* is not.

2. Excess: The word must modify *power* and be consistent with the idea of a lot of extra power: only *excess* (beyond what it necessary) fits those criteria.

3. Effects: *The* comes right before the word, making *effects* the only option.

4. A part: logically, Palmyra Atoll belongs to, i.e. is *a part of*, the Pacific Remote Islands Marine National Monument. In addition, something stands *apart FROM* but is *a part OF*. Since the word is followed by *of*, a *part* is required.

5. Averse: Based on the fact that Houdini *sought to conceal his inventive nature*, the word must help convey that Houdini avoided doing anything that would reveal his secrets. *Averse to* means "wanting to avoid," which is consistent with that idea.

6. Adhere: Logically, the sentence must be discussing the percentage of patients that follow, i.e. *adhere to*, their care plans.

7. Prosecuted: The passage indicates that federal authorities brought legal charges against Capone—that is, they *prosecuted* him.

8. Accept: The fact that Douglass struggled against slavery indicates that he refused to give into, i.e. *accept*, his situation. *Except* means "excluding" and does not make sense here.

9. Access: The fact that the Princeton Plasma Physics Laboratory is allowing students to work with equipment remotely indicates that those students are being given *access to* (that is, the right to use) that equipment. *Excess* means "too much" and does not make sense at all here.

10. Undertook…Effect: The passage indicates that Fornasier designed a creative scientific task in order to produce a particular result. The description of that task is consistent with the idea that he *undertook* it. *Overtake* would imply that Fornasier surpassed someone else in a competition, and there is no mention of that in the passage. For the second word, *effect* is correct because the word follows *the* (*the correct effect*).

Independent Practice #3: Wrong Connotation

1. B

The passage indicates that the Huygens probe was acquiring data to send back to scientists on Earth, so the correct word must mean something like "collected." *Stacked up* is a general synonym, but it is far too casual, so A) can be eliminated. *Hoarded* implies that the probe was keeping all the data for itself, which is the opposite of what the passage indicates. B) can thus be eliminated as well. *Convened* means "brought together" and is usually used in context of people gathering for a meeting or conference, so D) does not fit either. That leaves B): *gathered* is a moderately formal synonym for *collected*.

2. A

The fact that *humans consume only a fraction of the [citrus] varieties in existence* implies that only a few dozen citrus fruits have achieved commercial success. The correct word must therefore mean something like "achieved." *Racked up* and *snagged* are both far too casual, so B) and C) can be eliminated. D), *actualized*, is overly technical and means something closer to "brought about," which does not fit here. *Attained* is a moderately formal synonym for *achieved* and correctly conveys the idea that only a few citrus fruits are popular today.

3. D

In context of the examples in the last two sentences, the correct word must mean something like "figure out" or "determine." A), *engage* and B), *portray*, do not make sense at all, and C), *check out*, is far too casual. That leaves D), which fits: *assess* is a general synonym for *figure out*.

All Question Types: #1

1. B

The date *1999* indicates that the passage is referring to the year when the Savannah Bee Company was established, and *to found* means "to establish." The past form is *founded*, meaning that either A) or B) must be correct. *Principal* is an adjective meaning "primary" or "most important," but here a noun meaning something like "concept" is needed. Only *principle* fits that requirement, making B) correct.

2. A

Based on the context, the correct word must be a way to describe having a sensation of envy. Both *heap* and *stack* are far too casual, and *accretion* is too formal and does not have the correct connotation (an accretion is something that is built up by having parts stuck onto it). *Surge* (rush) is an acceptable way to describe a sudden emotion, making A) correct.

3. B

Illicit is an adjective meaning "illegal" or "not permitted," whereas the correct answer must be a verb meaning "produce" or "evoke." That is the definition of *elicit*, so B) is the best fit. C) is incorrect because to *extract* something is to physically pull it out of another object, a meaning that does not make sense here. Likewise, *compress* means "to bind or constrict," a definition that is inconsistent with the idea of musical notes producing colored visions in people with synesthesia.

4. C

The correct word must be a noun because it is preceded by *a* (*a permanent effect*). *Affect* is a verb and cannot be modified by the adjective *permanent*, so A) is incorrect. In addition to the fact that the adjective is *effective*, not *affective*, B) is wordy and awkward, and the construction *affective to* is not idiomatic. D) is incorrect because *effect* is a noun, and a verb must follow *would*. C) is correct because the adverb *permanently* appropriately modifies the verb *affect* and creates a logical meaning.

5.1 C

The passage states that *few distributors* accepted bitcoins, implying that the currency was difficult for users to get their hands on, i.e. *obtain*. It does not make sense to say that they could not *attain* (achieve) bitcoins. *Retain* would imply that bitcoin users could not get rid of their bitcoins, whereas the passage implies the opposite when it states that *only a small number of merchants accepted them. Contain* would imply that bitcoins users could not keep their money under control, an idea that is unsupported by the passage and that does not make a lot of sense.

5.2 A

The correct word must be a verb that corresponds to the subject *merchants*. It must also be consistent with the idea that bitcoins were difficult to use. *Accept* is a verb with the correct meaning. Logically, bitcoins were impractical because few merchants were willing/able to receive them. B) and C) use the homophone *except*, which means "without" and which does not make sense in this context. Likewise, D), *expecting*, makes far less sense than *accepted*. It also creates a grammatically unacceptable construction.

6.1 B

Access means "the ability to obtain," whereas *excess* means "more than what is necessary." Only the first word makes sense in context of the discussion of passwords and computer files, making C) and D) correct. A) is incorrect as well because one gains access *to* something, not access *of* something.

6.2 C

Along means "beside" or "next to," whereas the passage calls for an adjective describing *way*, i.e. a *long* way. That eliminates A) and B). D) is also incorrect because this answer creates an ungrammatical construction (*a long way ensuring*) when it is plugged into the sentence. The word *toward* is required, making C) correct.

7.1 C

The passage implies that Jansson is upset that an important aspect of her work has been ignored, so the correct word must mean something like "ignored." *Omitted* means "left out," which does not have the right connotation. A piece of information can be omitted from a document, but the same cannot really be said for an aspect of an artist's work. *Undone* means "taken apart," which does not make sense here; neither does *deleted*, which means "taken out of." That leaves *overlooked*, which means "(accidentally) ignored" and makes sense in context. C) is thus correct.

7.2 B

Imminent means "about to occur," a definition that cannot describe a person. A much more logical descriptor is *eminent*, which means "important" and is consistent with the idea that Jansson grew up in an environment in which artistic success was expected. *Big-time* has the right meaning but is far too casual, and *conspicuous* means "obvious" or "standing out," which is not the right connotation.

8.1 D

Given the context of the Mayo Clinic, the word in question is clearly intended to refer to people seeking medical treatment, i.e. *patients*. (*Patience* means "waiting without complaint.") D) is the only answer to include the correct form, so it must be correct by default. The different constructions in A)-C) are distractions.

8.2 C

This question tests two different sets of homophones simultaneously. To simplify things, start by considering each pair separately. Logically, the phrase is saying that employees are expected to accept the rule that patients are of primary importance. The first word must therefore mean something like "go along with," and the second word must mean something like "rule." *Cohere* means "hold together logically," which does not fit. An argument can cohere or not cohere, but a person must *adhere* to a rule. That eliminates A) and B). Next, *principal* can either mean "most important" or "head of a school," neither of which fits here. D) can be eliminated. In C), *principle* is similar to *rule* and is a much more logical fit for the sentence.

9.1 A

The passage is clearly talking about future events, as indicated by the phrase *In the next few decades*. In contrast, *precede* refers to something that came <u>before</u>. As a result, C) and D) can be eliminated. B) can be eliminated as well because it creates an ungrammatical construction when plugged back into the sentence. (Note: be careful not to mentally insert the word *of* after *transformation*, which would make this answer grammatically acceptable, if wordy and awkward.) That leaves A), which correctly uses *proceed* and employs a short, clear construction.

9.2 D

Given the context of car manufacturing, *corroborate* (support, prove) does not make a lot of sense. A much more logical meaning is that engineers must work together, i.e. *collaborate* to produce new parts. A) and B) can thus be eliminated. C) can be eliminated as well because *collaborate* must be followed by *on* here; it is grammatically unacceptable for a noun to be placed immediately afterward. That leaves D), which is correct.

10.1 A

Based on the context of the passage, the word in question must refer to people who want to become interns, i.e. *prospective* interns. *Perspective* means "point of view," and *perceptive* describes someone with a highly developed ability to notice detail, so B) and D) can be eliminated. B) is incorrect because *by prospective interns* implies that the potential interns are the ones giving the tours. Logically, however, prospective interns would be given tours by current IBM employees. That eliminates B), leaving A).

10.2 B

The passage is comparing P-tech graduates to graduates of traditional programs. *Than*, not *then*, should always be used to form comparisons, so B) is correct.

10.3 A

The correct word follows *a* (*a significant _____*), so the noun *effect* is required. That makes A) the only possible answer.

All Question Types: Set #2

1. C

Respectably means "in a respectable (socially acceptable) manner;" *respectfully* means "in a respectful manner;" and *effectively* means "in an effective" manner." None of those words makes sense in context. A far more logical word is *respectively*, which serves to make clear that 68% of the universe is composed of dark energy, and 27% of the universe is made up of dark matter. C) is thus correct.

2. D

Censured means punished, something that can only be done to a person or group of people. A much more logical meaning is that Cerf and his colleagues are attempting to prevent information from being *censored*—that is, blocked or partially reported in order to eliminate controversial or offensive viewpoints. D) is the only answer that includes the correct version of this word, so it must be correct. The different constructions in A)-C) are simply a distraction.

3. D

Aspire means "strive" or "have the goal of achieving." Here, however, the correct word must be similar to "cause." Only *inspire* is consistent with that definition, eliminating A) and B). Even though C) provides the correct version of the word, this answer does not make grammatical sense when it is plugged into the sentence. D) contains the correct version of the word and creates a clear and logical construction, making it correct.

4.1 B

Logically, the correct word must mean something like "improve." To *uphold* something is to keep it at its existing (high) level, not to improve it, so A) can be eliminated. *Rev up* means "energize" and is far too informal, so C) can be eliminated. D), *reform*, is used to describe someone who has abandoned a life of crime or corruption, a meaning that does not make sense here at all. The most appropriate word is *bolstered*, which fits as a straightforward synonym for *improved*.

4.2 C

Given that the passage offers no indication that the workers have been poisoned, a discussion of *antidotes* (medicines that can counteract toxic substance) would make no sense. In contrast, it is entirely reasonable that these workers would swap *anecdotes*, or stories. A) and B) can thus be eliminated. D) can be eliminated as well because it can be reasonably assumed that the workers are sharing stories with one another *over* a cup of coffee, not that workers are sharing their stories *with* a cup of coffee.

5.1 C

Logically, the sentence is intending to say that the *Tribune* played a role, i.e. *a part*, in Lincoln's election. *Apart* means "separate from" and does not make sense in context, so A) and B) can be eliminated. D) can also be eliminated because *a part* must be followed by *in*. That leaves C), which correctly uses *a part* to indicate that the *Tribune* played a role in making Lincoln President.

5.2 A

The correct word must indicate that the *Tribune* played a large part in getting businesses to move to Chicago after the fire of 1871. Logically, it must mean something like "attract." *Chase, trap*, and *snare* all have distinctly negative connotations, whereas *lure* is more positive and implies that the *Tribune* portrayed Chicago in a flattering light in order to make businesses want to set up shop there. A) is thus correct.

6.1 C

Cohere means "hold together logically," which does not quite fit here. An argument can cohere, but a machine "learning" to identify patterns in data must follow, or *adhere to*, those patterns. That eliminates A) and B). D) does not fit either because *cling to* would imply that the computer was physically holding onto something rather than acquiring pattern-recognition skills.

6.2 A

Effective is the adjective form of *effect* and refers to something that has a strong impact. Here, it implies that the web searches permitted by machine learning are successful—a logical meaning given the passage's discussion of inventions made possible by machine learning. A) is thus correct. *Affective* does exist (it means "causing emotions"), but the chance of it appearing as a correct answer on the SAT is virtually zero. *Affectionate* means "having great tenderness toward," which does not make sense at all. That eliminates C). *Infectious* describes something that spreads easily, e.g. a virus, so D) clearly does not fit either. A) is thus correct.

7.1 A

Logically, the correct word must mean something like "revealed." *Imported* is a word often associated with food, but it refers to bringing crops and goods in from a different place, not to informing consumers about the contents of their food. B) can be thus be eliminated. *Blabbed about* is far, far too slangy and casual, so C) can eliminated as well. D) is incorrect because *uncovered* implies that the ingredients are literally being hidden from view. A) is correct because in standard English, information is *disclosed* in order to inform the public about health-related issues.

7.2 B

The fact that the type of gene editing described in the passage *falls outside of current regulations* indicates that consumers will be unable to determine whether foods contain affected ingredients. As a result, it is reasonable to assume that these foods will *escape* consumers' detection. *Allude* means "refer to," which does not make sense at all. C), *confound*, means "confuse," which does not make sense either. D), *run away from*, does not have the right connotation (foods cannot "run away from" anything) and is far too casual. *Elude* means "avoid" or "evade" and correctly describes foods that will remain undetectable, making B) correct.

8.1 C

Prosecuted refers to the act of charging a person with a crime, and that is not the case here. A much more logical scenario here is that Cinderella's stepmother *persecuted* (harassed, punished) her out of envy. The only possible options are therefore C) and D). D) does not make sense because a person can be persecuted *for* a belief or a physical characteristic, but here the implication is that the stepmother is the one doing the persecuting—that is, the heroine is persecuted *by* her stepmother. That leaves C), which is correct.

8.2 B

Implicit describes something that is implied or understood without being directly stated, a meaning that does not make sense in the case of talking animals. A) can thus be eliminated. A much more logical meaning is that the magical plants and talking animals are *complicit* in the heroine's escape— that is, they help her to escape. C), *complied with* ("went along with"), does not make grammatical sense: someone can comply with a rule or an order, but it is unacceptable to say that the plants/animals *are complied with* the heroine's escape. D) is incorrect because *complicated* implies exactly the opposite of what the passage is saying: the plants and animals aid in Cinderella's escape rather than make it harder. B) is the only answer that is both grammatical and logical, so it is correct.

9.1 B

The passage indicates that cycling enthusiasts have mixed feelings about e-bikes: they enjoy the higher speeds but find the experience lacking and the bikes clunky. In other words, they are *ambivalent*. A meaning can be *ambiguous*, but a person can only be *ambivalent*. C), *hazy*, is too casual, and neither it nor D), *vague*, conveys the idea of having mixed feelings. B) is thus correct.

9.2 C

Used to, not *use to*, means "accustomed to," and the passage indicates that serious cyclists do not like e-bikes in part because they are *accustomed to* lightweight frames. That eliminates A) and makes C) the answer. B) is incorrect because it makes no sense to say that the cyclists are used *as* lightweight frames. Clearly, a person cannot be a bike frame! D), *using to*, creates an ungrammatical construction, eliminating that answer as well.

10.1 D

The passage is describing devices that are surgically placed in the brain, so the correct word must refer to that action. A), *supplanted*, means "replaced by force," and B) *implemented* means "put into effect," neither of which fits. In contrast, *implanted* accurately describes the act of placing something into a person's body, so C) or D) must be correct. C) can be eliminated because to say that memory chips are implanted *by* the brain is to say that the brain does the implanting itself. Clearly, that is impossible. D) correctly indicates that the chips are placed *in* the brain, a much more logical meaning.

10.2 A

To *simulate* is to create a model of something, or to give the impression of something being real, but that definition does not make sense here. B) and C) can thus be eliminated. Likewise, to *emulate* something is to copy it, which does not make sense here either. D) can thus be eliminated. *Stimulating* correctly conveys the idea that the device causes the brain to form memories, so A) is correct.

10.3 C

Based on the context, the correct word must be a synonym for *affected (by)*. The only answer to match that definition is C), *afflicted*. It possible to *inflict* pain or illness on a person, but a person cannot be *inflicted with* or *inflicted by*, eliminating A) and B). *Conflicted* means "torn" or "having mixed feelings," a definition that does not fit at all and that makes D) incorrect as well.

Chapter 4: Transitional Words and Phrases

How many times have you used the words *for example* and *however* in your essays for school? Most writers use these common words on a regular basis. Now, let us ask you another question: How many times have you used the words *in fact*, *conversely*, and *consequently* in your essays? You probably use these words a lot less frequently than you use *for example* and *however*.

For example, *however*, *in fact*, *conversely*, and *consequently* are all transitional words. A transition is a change or shift, and that is exactly the function these words perform in a sentence. They signal a change or a shift in an author's presentation of thoughts.

College Board test writers are aware of the important role transitional words play in good writing. That's why the SAT Writing and Language test typically includes 4-6 questions designed to test your understanding of transitional words and phrases.

We have good news and bad news about transitional words. The good news is that the College Board draws its correct answers from a pool of only about 25 words. The bad news is that you must have a precise understanding of what these words mean and how they are used in sentences.

Dwayne "the Rock" Johnson to the Rescue

Is it possible for Dwayne "the Rock" Johnson to help you deliver a "people's elbow" to the SAT transitional questions? At first glance, this is an absurd question. After all, Johnson is a former wrestling champion and a current action adventure movie star. Wouldn't a detailed glossary of terms be more helpful than the Rock's "people's elbow?" Before you dismiss Johnson as an irrelevant distraction, bear with us and read the following passage about him.

Dwayne "The Rock" Johnson is now one of the world's best-known and most highly paid celebrities. He is a former WWE wrestling champion and a star in the hugely successful *Fast and Furious* movie franchise. **In addition**, *People Magazine* named Johnson 2016's "World's Sexiest Man."

Success has not always come easily to Johnson. As a promising football player at the University of Miami, Johnson hoped to have a professional career playing in the NFL. **However**, an injury ended his dream and left him dejected and impoverished. "I looked in my pocket," Johnson remembers, "and I had seven bucks to my name."

Today, Johnson oversees an entertainment company appropriately named Seven Bucks Productions. He is busy writing a second autobiography, preparing new movie projects, and creating a YouTube channel. Johnson's popularity is soaring. He is a charismatic entertainer with a global reach that extends to more than 100 million followers on various platforms. **Accordingly**, Johnson is now shifting his attention to foreign markets because he knows the pivotal role they play in the successful career of a contemporary movie star.

The short passage on the previous page contains interesting details about Johnson's career. Each paragraph features a key transitional word that directs the flow of ideas. In the first paragraph, the transitional phrase *in addition* continues the writer's line of thought by providing another example of why Johnson is one of the world's *best known and most highly paid celebrities*.

The second paragraph also uses a key transitional word. Did you notice how the word *however* signals a reversal in the sequence of events in Johnson's career? It provides a contrast between Johnson's hopes for a professional football career and the disastrous impact of his injury.

Finally, the third paragraph uses the transitional word *accordingly* to logically connect two thoughts. The paragraph begins by describing Johnson's current activities and soaring popularity. We learn that he has over 100 million followers. So how will he use his popularity? The transitional word *accordingly* captures the cause-and-effect relationship between Johnson's popularity and his goal of reaching an international market.

Types and Importance of Transitional Relationships

The words *in addition, however,* and *accordingly* illustrate three basic transitional relationships tested in the SAT Writing and Language section.

- *In addition* and words like *for example* are part of a group of transitional words that signal a **continuation** or extension of a thought.

- *However* and words like *instead* and *conversely* are part of a group of transitional words that signal a **reversal** or **contrast** between two thoughts.

- *Accordingly* and words like *therefore* and *consequently* are part of a group of transitional words that signal a **cause-and-effect relationship** between two thoughts.

The 4-5 transition questions comprise the largest single cluster of items on the Writing and Language test. Taken together, they are worth about 10% of your Writing and Language score.

The chart on the following page provides a list of common transitions along with their purposes.

Common Transitions

Continue	Cause-and-Effect	Reverse
Add Information And Also Furthermore In addition Moreover **Give Example** For example For instance **Define** That is **Emphasize** In fact Indeed **Compare** Likewise Similarly **Order of Events** Next Then Subsequently Finally Ultimately	Accordingly As a result As As such Because Consequently Since So Thereby Thus Therefore	Alternately Alternatively (Al)though But Conversely Despite Even so Even though However In contrast In spite of Instead Meanwhile Nevertheless Nonetheless Otherwise On the contrary On the other hand Rather Still Whereas While Yet

How to Answer Transition Questions

We will examine each of the three transitional relationships in much greater detail. But first, let's take a detailed look at the steps you should follow to answer transition questions.

Consider the following example:

1.   Harold Garfinkle, a leader in the field of ethnomethodology, has developed a number of techniques for uncovering hidden social patterns. In one experiment, Garfinkle's students deliberately injected confusion into casual conversations. However, when asked, "How are you?" one student unexpectedly replied: "How am I in regard to what? My health, my finances, my peace of mind?"

A) NO CHANGE
B) Alternatively,
C) Accordingly,
D) For example,

Step 1: Cross out the transitional word or phrase

As soon as you encounter a transition question, use your pencil to cross out the underlined phrase or word. Transition questions are about what words mean, not how they sound in a sentence. A word that sounds fine to you might create a completely illogical relationship. Crossing out the original phrase or word will make it easier for you to focus on what each sentence is saying. So begin our sample example by crossing out the word *however*.

> ~~However,~~ when asked, "How are you?" one student unexpectedly replied: "How am I in regard to what? My health, my finances, my peace of mind?"

To reiterate: you must physically pick up your pencil and draw a line through the word. Do not just cross it out mentally. Otherwise, you may develop an unconscious bias toward the original word in the passage, regardless of whether it actually makes sense.

Step 2: Identify the type of relationship between the relevant sentences

SAT authors use transitional phrases and words to continue thoughts, contrast thoughts, or establish a causal relationship between two thoughts. So consider the two relevant thoughts back-to-back:

Sentence 1:   In one experiment, Garfinkle's students deliberately injected confusion into casual conversations.

Sentence 2:   When asked, "How are you?" one student unexpectedly replied: "How am I in regard to what? My health, my finances, my peace of mind?"

In the first sentence, we learn that Garfinkle's students deliberately caused confusion. The second sentence describes how the students caused confusion (they responded to a common question in an unusual way). Those are similar ideas, and the transition must reflect that fact.

Step 3: Narrow Your Choices

Now that you know what you're looking for, you can eliminate choices that don't make logical connections.

1

    A) NO CHANGE
    B) Alternatively,
    C) Accordingly,
    D) For example,

Choices A), *However*, and B), *Alternatively*, both express a contrast or reversal and can be eliminated. **Note that if two or more answers express the same relationship, both answers can be crossed out because no question can have more than one correct answer.** Choice C), *Accordingly*, can also be eliminated since it expresses a causal relationship that is not called for in our example.

STEP 4: Choose the Correct Answer

Choice D), *For example*, accurately continues the relationship between our key sentences by indicating a specific way in which Garfinkle's students disrupt casual conversations. Now that you have chosen a correct answer, be sure to accurately bubble it in on your answer sheet!

A Closer Look at Continuation Words

Continuers are transitional words that add information, introduce examples, emphasize key points, and elaborate on a preceding point. They are the most frequently tested type of transitional words, comprising just over half of all transition questions. This should not come as a surprise because the new SAT is designed to test your ability to identify and provide different types of evidence. These words lead the reader to additional evidence.

A. Key Words and Key Points

1. FOR EXAMPLE and FOR INSTANCE

Both phrases indicate that a relevant example will follow. They lead the reader to specific examples that support a previous point or claim. Note that *for example* and *for instance* are the most frequently tested continuers.

2. IN FACT, INDEED, IN PARTICULAR, and TO THESE ENDS

These phrases and words add emphasis to a previous statement. *In fact* and *indeed* are the second most frequently tested continuers.

3. IN ADDITION, ALSO, MOREOVER, FURTHERMORE, and BESIDES

These phrases and words signal that the next sentence will add another example or point. It is important to note that *besides* is often used as a wrong answer.

4. SIMILARLY, LIKEWISE, and BY THE SAME TOKEN

The words and phrases mean "in the same way." They continue an argument by making a comparison between two points.

5. SUBSEQUENTLY

This word indicates that an action or event logically follows another action or event. You should be able to substitute *next* and *then* to confirm that *subsequently* is correct.

B. Guided Practice: Continuation Questions

Example #1

1. String theory is a broad theoretical framework that addresses a number of questions about nature's most fundamental constituents and forces. Alternatively, scientists are applying string theory to problems such as early universe cosmology, black hole physics, and the varieties of particle ingredients.

1

A) NO CHANGE
B) By contrast,
C) However,
D) For instance,

The correct answer is D). *For instance* signals continuation by introducing a list of specific examples that illustrate how string theory *addresses a number of questions about nature's most fundamental constituents and forces.* Answer choices A), B), and C) can be eliminated since all three are reversal words.

Example #2:

2.   Sociologists Robert and Helen Lynd opened an office in a small Midwestern town they referred to as "Middletown" and spent the next 18 months gathering data. During this time, the Lynds participated as fully as possible in all phases of community life. **2** Conversely, they examined documentary materials, compiled statistical tables, conducted interviews, and administered questionnaires.

2

A) NO CHANGE
B) In addition,
C) However,
D) Despite this,

The correct answer is B). *In addition* signals continuation by introducing a list of examples that illustrate how Robert and Helen Lynd studied community life. Answer choices A), C), and D) can be eliminated since they are all reversal words.

Example #3

3.   Suzanne Bell, a psychologist at DePaul University, has been attempting to determine how NASA can create the most effective team for a long-term mission to Mars. One of her discoveries is that people with more outgoing personalities may not be particularly well suited to such a mission. Spacecraft simulations have revealed that extroverted team members are likely to be ostracized by other members who were are reserved. **3** In other words, extroverts may have a hard time adjusting to environments where there's little opportunity for new activities or social interactions, the researchers said.

3

A) NO CHANGE
B) Therefore,
C) Moreover,
D) Hence,

The correct answer is C). The sentence begun by the transition introduces a new point supporting the idea that extroverts are not well suited for travel to Mars. Choices B) and D) can be eliminated immediately because they have the same meaning, and no question can have more than one correct answer. Choice A) can be eliminated because it does not restate or clarify the previous point.

Example #4

4.   On December 1, 1955, a Montgomery bus driver ordered Rosa Parks to give up her seat to a white passenger. Even though Parks knew that her actions would undoubtedly result in a fine and a night in jail, she did not waver. In a calm and steady voice, she answered with just one word: "No!" **4** Subsequently, Parks' courageous action inspired outraged African Americans led by her minister, Dr. Martin Luther King, Jr., to boycott the Montgomery buses.

4

A) NO CHANGE
B) Previously,
C) Instead,
D) However,

The correct answer is A). *Subsequently* signals that the Montgomery bus boycott occurred **after** Parks refused to give up her seat. That makes sense because it is logical to assume that Parks's decision inspired the boycott. Choices B), C), and D) do not establish this relationship.

A Closer Look at Reversal Words

Reversals are words that introduce a contradiction, limitation, conflicting idea or alternative. They are the second most frequently tested type of transitional word and comprise about one-third of all transition questions.

A. Key Words and Key Points

1. HOWEVER and ALTHOUGH

These key words signal an exception to a point stated in a preceding sentence. Be alert for a contrast between two thoughts. *However* is by far the most frequently tested reversal word. It comprises about two-thirds of all the questions testing reversal words.

2. INSTEAD

This commonly used word means "in place of" or "a substitute for." Although *instead* is often used as a wrong answer, it has on very rare occasions also been correct.

3. CONVERSELY, IN CONTRAST, and ON THE OTHER HAND

Both words introduce a statement or idea that reverses one that has just been made or referred to. They signal that the author's thoughts will move in a contrary or opposite direction.

4. DESPITE

This reversal word means "in spite of." For example, we won the game *despite* facing overwhelming odds.

5. NONETHELESS, NEVERTHELESS, and NOTWITHSTANDING

All three are interchangeable synonyms meaning "despite this" or "however."

6. ALTERNATIVELY

Signals the presentation of another option or different choice.

B. Guided Practice: Reversal Questions

Example #5

5. At the time of the Trojan War, sometime around the twelfth century B.C.E., aristocratic women led lives of relative independence. **5** For example, centuries later women in Greek cities lived under severe constraints.

5
A) NO CHANGE
B) In fact,
C) However,
D) Moreover,

The correct answer is C). *However* signals a reversal or contrast to the situation described in the first sentence. The phrase *severe constraints* sets up a contrast with the *relative independence* previously enjoyed by women during the Homeric period. Choices A), B), and D) can be eliminated because they indicate a continuation that is not justified by the passage.

Example #6

6. Hokusai moved away from the tradition of making images of affluent courtesans and actors who were the customary subject of *ukiyo-e* prints. **6** Similarly, his work focused on the daily life of everyday Japanese people from all walks of life.

6

A) NO CHANGE
B) Instead,
C) For example,
D) Without doubt,

The correct answer is B). *Instead* signals a reversal or contrast between the traditional affluent subjects of *ukiyo-e* art and the new everyday people whom Hokusai chose to portray. Choices A), C), and D) do not signal this contrast.

Example #7

7. The 1950s offered two contrasting lifestyles. Prizing conformity and material comfort, many Americans chose to live in the nation's new suburbs. **7** Alternatively, a small but influential group of Beats rejected the "square" suburban lifestyle and chose to live spontaneous lives in urban enclaves such as Greenwich Village in New York City.

7

A) NO CHANGE
B) Also,
C) For instance,
D) Consequently,

The correct answer is A). *Alternatively* signals a contrast between the suburban lifestyle and the Beat lifestyle. Choices B) and C) can be eliminated because they both signal a continuation that is not present in the example. Choice D) can be eliminated because it signals a cause-and-effect relationship that is not present in the example.

A Closer Look at Cause-and-Effect Words

Cause-and-effect words signal a causal relationship between two thoughts. They are the least frequently tested type of transition, comprising about one-eighth of all transition questions.

A. Key Words and Key Points

1. CONSEQUENTLY, THEREFORE, THUS, and HENCE

All signal a logical cause-and-effect relationship between two thoughts. You should be able to substitute the phrase *as a result* to confirm that any of these words is the correct answer. Note that *consequently* is the most frequently tested cause-and-effect word.

2. ACCORDINGLY

Refers to a thought or action that is logically appropriate to a given circumstance.

B. Guided Practice: Cause-and-Effect Questions

Example #8

8.   Steve Jobs was an aggressive and demanding chief executive who was known for his exacting standards and painstaking attention to detail. **8** Previously, Jobs had little tolerance for mediocre employees or inferior products.

8
- A) NO CHANGE
- B) Despite this,
- C) However,
- D) Consequently,

The correct answer is D). Logically, the fact that Jobs had *little tolerance for mediocre people or inferior products* was the result of his *exacting standards and painstaking attention to detail*. Choices A), B), and C) do not establish this cause-and-effect relationship.

Example #9

9.   The Tiger of Ch'in unified China in 221 B.C. and took the title Ch'in Shih Huang-ti or First Emperor. The ruthless First Emperor feared just one thing—death. He regularly left his palaces to search for the means to immortality. **9** Regardless, he consulted sorcerers, made sacrifices to numerous deities, and drank what he hoped were life-preserving elixirs.

9
- A) NO CHANGE
- B) Nevertheless,
- C) Accordingly,
- D) Similarly,

The correct answer is C). *Accordingly* signals a cause-and-effect relationship between the First Emperor's fear of death and his quest for immortality. Choices A), B), and D) do not establish this cause-and-effect relationship.

Transition Placement

As we've seen, transition questions often involve a transitional word at the beginning of a sentence or clause—that is, the transitional word will follow a period or a semicolon, as in the sentences below.

> When it comes to novels, there's no precise formula for an iconic opening sentence. Herman Melville kept his first lines **short. However,** Jane Austen was known to begin her novels with an entire paragraph.

> When it comes to novels, there's no precise formula for an iconic opening sentence. Herman Melville kept his first lines **short; however,** Jane Austen w as known to begin her novels with an entire paragraph.

On the SAT, transitional words and phrases may also be placed between two commas in the middle of a sentence.

> When it comes to novels, there's no precise formula for an iconic opening sentence. Herman Melville kept his first lines short. Jane Austen**, however,** was known to begin her novels with an entire paragraph.

The most important thing to understand is that these two constructions are interchangeable. Either way, the transition is used to indicate a sentence's relationship to the <u>previous</u> sentence.

As a result, you should treat "two comma" transition questions exactly like other transition questions: cross out the transitional word or phrase; read the sentence in which it appears AND the previous sentence; determine the relationship (continue, reverse, cause-and-effect); and select your answer.

Consider the following example:

1. Europeans developed the process for making chocolate candies during the 1850s. Chocolatiers in Belgium played an important role in the development of the praline and other tasty treats. Within a short time, producing and consuming chocolate candies became a significant and enduring part of the Belgian economy and culture. **1** Shops featuring chocolate-filled display windows can, <u>in fact,</u> still be found across Belgium today.

1

A) NO CHANGE
B) however,
C) at any rate,
D) nevertheless,

The commas around the underlined transition tell us that it is necessary to back up and consider the relationship between the last sentence and the previous sentence.

The previous sentence tells us that the chocolate industry plays an important role in Belgian culture; the last sentence affirms that idea by indicating that chocolate stores are still found across Belgium.

Those are similar ideas, so *however* and *nevertheless* can be eliminated. *At any rate* means "in any case," which does not make sense in this context. That leaves A), which correctly indicates that the last sentence is emphasizing a point made in the previous sentence.

No Transition or DELETE Questions

Note: this type of question has only appeared twice on released SATs, but we are including it here for the sake of thoroughness.

On very rare occasions, you may encounter transition questions that include an answer without a transition, or an answer that gives you the possibility of deleting the transition.

When one of these options is present, you should make sure to check it *first*. Because this answer type is so unusual, its very appearance suggests that it has a better than average chance of being correct.

For example:

1. There are many parts of produce that consumers don't usually eat—apple cores, orange peels, carrot tops, cucumber ends. Therefore, these commonly trashed edibles are sometimes recycled by inventive chefs. In most developed nations, however, people waste a lot of food.

1

A) NO CHANGE
B) Hence,
C) Furthermore,
D) DELETE the underlined portion.

Don't get distracted by the transitional word *therefore* in the passage. Option D) provides a significant clue that a transition might not even be required. And in fact, the second sentence does not describe a logical result of the first sentence, as *therefore* and *hence* would imply. *Furthermore* does not make sense either, since the second sentence introduces a new idea rather than building on the previous one. As a result, the best option is to delete the transition entirely. D) is thus correct.

Independent Practice: Set #1

1. The American Museum of Natural History in New York City boasts one of the greatest collections of dinosaur fossils in the world. **1** Conversely, the collection includes a fearsome *Tyrannosaurus Rex* with 6-inch-long teeth and a 4-foot-long jaw.

1
A) NO CHANGE
B) Despite this,
C) Therefore,
D) For instance,

2. Stockbrokers who produce high returns for their clients attribute their success to dispositional factors, such as exhaustive research and disciplined investing. **2** Nevertheless, stockbrokers who produce low returns for their clients blame situational factors, such as unpredictable actions by foreign governments and surprise decisions by the Federal Reserve Board.

2
A) NO CHANGE
B) In addition,
C) Conversely,
D) Ironically,

3. Scientists have long known that genes control physical characteristics such as hair color and height. **3** Thus, recent research on identical twins provides evidence supporting the opposing view that nurture—our sociological history—also plays an integral role in our development.

3
A) NO CHANGE
B) Indeed,
C) Similarly,
D) However,

4. One of the most significant social changes of the Renaissance involved merchants' social status. In the past, many merchants had inherited their rank, but beginning in the fifteenth century, success in business began to depend on an entrepreneur's own wits. **4** Consequently, merchants took increasing pride in their work, believing that their achievements resulted from individual merit.

4
A) NO CHANGE
B) Nevertheless,
C) Previously,
D) However,

5. Elon Musk is visionary inventor and entrepreneur who is determined to create world-changing technologies. In 2008, **5** nevertheless, his company Tesla motors unveiled the world's first viable long-distance electric car, a vehicle that has the potential to end the automotive industry's harmful dependence on fossil fuels.

5
A) NO CHANGE
B) for example,
C) similarly,
D) however,

6. A typical business day in a large Japanese corporation usually includes a number of lengthy meetings. Individual participants do not claim credit for specific ideas or programs; **6** finally, they strive for group consensus. Once a decision is reached, it becomes the group's opinion.

6
A) NO CHANGE
B) for instance,
C) besides,
D) instead,

7. Speed reading programs focus on modifying readers' behavior in several ways. Remarkably, all of these ways were described in an obscure 1958 book, *Reading Skills*, by Evelyn Wood and Marjorie Barrows. Ironically, Wood and Barrows did not emphasize speed; **7** on the other hand, the term "speed reading" never even appears in their book. Despite this, their methods became the foundation for what is now known as speed reading.

7
A) NO CHANGE
B) however,
C) subsequently,
D) in fact,

8. Experts have suggested that quantum computers could break the toughest mainstream encryption strategies in use today. Increased processing speed will eventually allow them to crack codes that today are too difficult to unravel. Current commercial interest in quantum computing is, **8** then, primarily focused on the simpler task of helping analysts identify security incidents and determine which ones represent a true threat.

8
A) NO CHANGE
B) for instance,
C) however,
D) similarly,

9.   One of President John F. Kennedy's goals was to encourage national fitness. Shortly before taking office, Kennedy published an article in *Sports Illustrated* warning about the negative effects of a sedentary lifestyle. Two years later, he discovered an executive order from Theodore Roosevelt challenging U.S. Marine officers to finish a 50-mile march in less than twenty hours. **9** Subsequently, Kennedy passed the document on to his own Marine Commandant, suggesting that modern troops should duplicate this feat. Within a short time, the "Kennedy March" became a national challenge for Marines and the public at large.

9
A) NO CHANGE
B) Nevertheless,
C) However,
D) In particular,

10. Over the past several decades, it has become increasingly apparent that the burning of coal and other fossil fuels is shifting precipitation patterns, strengthening hurricanes, and melting polar ice caps. **10** However, toxic metals and other hazardous pollutants from coal-burning electric power plants are posing a greater and greater risk to the environment and to human health.

10
A) NO CHANGE
B) Moreover,
C) Conversely,
D) At any rate,

Independent Practice: Set #2

1. Distance running can cause micro-tears in muscle fibers, which trigger an inflammatory response. But help could be on the way from an unlikely source—tart cherry juice. Recent research has shown that the drink has powerful anti-inflammatory properties. Unfortunately, the studies are not conclusive. **1** Regardless, it is not clear why drinking cherry juice reduced pain but did not significantly affect range of motion.

1

A) NO CHANGE
B) In particular,
C) Nevertheless,
D) Even so,

2. Career experts predict that America's healthcare sector will rapidly expand during the coming decade. There will, **2** nevertheless, be a strong demand for registered nurses to assess the needs of and provide care for our aging populations.

2

A) NO CHANGE
B) however,
C) despite this,
D) consequently,

3. During the Middle Ages, architects sought to accomplish a seemingly impossible task: increase the height of churches while simultaneously allowing more light to enter their interior spaces. One possibility was to build thicker walls. **3** Alternatively, some architects believed they could use flying buttresses to support tall but thin walls that would provide increased space for stained-glass windows.

3

A) NO CHANGE
B) Consequently,
C) Hence,
D) Finally,

4. *Street Corner Society* has a remarkable dramatic quality; no other work of sociology contains so much skillful characterization and emotion. William F. Whyte did not pretend to study the established institutions of a city he called "Cornerville." **4** Nonetheless, he scarcely mentioned the family, the church, the schools, and the legitimate sector of the local economy. His exclusive topic of inquiry was the voluntary associations of a street corner gang called the Nortons.

4

A) NO CHANGE
B) In other words,
C) Indeed,
D) Likewise,

5. Katsushika Hokusai's *The Great Wave* has become one of the most famous works of art in the world—and debatably the most iconic work of Japanese art. Initially, thousands of copies of this print were quickly produced and sold cheaply. **5** As an additional benefit, it was created at a time when Japanese trade was heavily restricted, Hokusai's print displays the influence of Dutch art.

5

A) NO CHANGE
B) Because
C) Although
D) Besides,

6. On June 30, 1908, an unidentified object exploded near the Tunguska River in remote Siberia, destroying eighty million trees. Locals reported seeing something blue streak across the sky. **6** Subsequently, they heard a tremendous crash and felt the earth tremble. Scientists speculate that a 220-million pound asteroid had entered the atmosphere above Siberia. But why did it explode in the air? And why haven't researchers or the public found any pieces?

6

A) NO CHANGE
B) Likewise,
C) In sharp contrast,
D) Yet,

7. Around the middle of the nineteenth century, new printing technology and political conditions paved the way for the affordable daily newspaper, the world's first mass medium. This new form of publication spread quickly throughout Europe. In 1850, one in nine Germans read a paper. Forty years later, **7** therefore, the number was one in two. The newspaper market soon became highly fragmented and diverse, not unlike today's infinite playground of cable channels and Internet outlets.

7

A) NO CHANGE
B) in fact,
C) furthermore,
D) however,

8. The invention of photography irrevocably changed art. Soon after the first photographic portraits appeared, critics and artists began to predict that portrait painting would eventually become obsolete. **8** Despite this, within three generations after the invention of photography, artists abandoned realistic images for abstract works.

8

A) NO CHANGE
B) In fact,
C) Nevertheless,
D) Thus,

9. Unleashing new kinds of artificial intelligence (AI) on mountains of patient data will change the medical world in fundamental ways. **9** Therefore, AI will speed up diagnoses and get patients on the path to recovery much sooner. It also promises to dramatically change the job description for doctors who identify as information specialists—those whose primary tasks involve deciphering diagnoses from images.

9

A) NO CHANGE
B) As a result,
C) However,
D) DELETE the underlined portion

10. Now that scientists have sequenced the genome of the *Coffea arabica* coffee plant—the species that makes up the vast majority of global production—genes have become the future of coffee. In the coming years, breeders will use the information to develop plant varieties that improve on existing ones. Some of these plants might, **10** however, have new flavors; others could have better resistance to cold and disease.

A) NO CHANGE
B) as a rule,
C) for instance,
D) nevertheless,

Answers: Transitions Independent Practice

Set #1

1. D

The first sentence makes a general statement regarding the exceptional nature of the Museum of Natural History's dinosaur fossil collection, and the second sentence uses the example of the *Tyrannosaurus Rex* to illustrate that idea. *For instance* is the only answer that can be used to introduce an example, making D) correct. *Conversely* and *Despite this* indicate a reversal, eliminating A) and B). *Therefore* indicates a cause-and-effect relationship, eliminating C).

2. C

The question asks you to work with two fairly long sentences, but you can answer the question most easily by focusing on the big picture: the first sentence discusses stockbrokers who produce high returns, whereas the second sentence discusses stockbrokers who produce low returns. Those are contrasting ideas, so a transition indicating a reversal is required. Neither *In addition* nor *Ironically* indicates a contrast, so A) and D) can be eliminated. *Nevertheless* means "despite this," which does not fit either, so B) can be eliminated as well. The transition that captures that straightforward contrast most effectively is *Conversely*, making C) correct.

3. D

The two sentences provide opposing ideas: the first sentence focuses on the role of genes in influencing identity, whereas the second sentence focuses on the role of nurture (environment). *Thus* indicates a cause-and-effect relationship, so A) can be eliminated. *Indeed* and *Similarly* are both used to continue ideas, so B) and C) can be eliminated. That leaves *However*, which correctly sets up the contrast between the two sentences and makes D) correct.

4. A

The first two sentences of the passage indicate that during the Renaissance, merchants began to view their success as something that came from their own efforts rather than something that was merely inherited. In other words, their increasing pride in their work was the *result* of their own wits. That's a cause-and-effect relationship. *Consequently* is the only answer to indicate that relationship, so A) is correct.

5. B

Remember that even though the underlined transition is not the first word in the sentence, it is still used to indicate that sentence's relationship to the previous sentence. The previous sentence presents a main idea (Musk is a visionary who wants to create world-changing technologies), and the sentence in question provides a specific example of a potentially world-changing technology created by Musk (*the world's first viable long-distance car*). *For example* is therefore the most appropriate transitional word, making B) correct. A) and D) do not fit because *nevertheless* and *however* are used to introduce contrasting information. C), *similarly*, does not fit because the second sentence does not introduce a new piece of similar evidence. Rather, it signals a move from a general statement to specific example.

6. D

The two halves of the sentence express opposing ideas: the first half describes what participants don't do (take personal credit for ideas), whereas the second half describes what they do (strive for group consensus). Those are contrasting ideas, so a transitional word indicating a reversal is required. The only answer to match that requirement is *instead*, making D) correct. The other answers are all continuers.

7. B

This has the potential to be a very tricky question, but you can use the answer choices to guide you. *On the other hand* and *however* have very similar meanings, so you can assume both A) and B) are incorrect. (Remember that two answers with the same meaning can be eliminated automatically because no question can have more than one correct answer.) *Subsequently* means "next," which does not make sense here: the transition is not introducing an action that followed an earlier action. C) can thus be eliminated as well. So by process of elimination, B) must be correct.

Now, why is B) correct? Because the point of the passage is that Wood's and Barrows's book became the basis for speed reading, even though it was not intended to teach that skill. The two pieces of information before and after the semicolon are both intended to support the irony of that fact. The second piece of information—the information introduced by the transition—builds on the previous statement by emphasizing that *Reading Skills* was not intended to teach speed reading.

8. C

Remember that even though the transition appears in the middle of the sentence, it is still used to indicate that sentence's relationship to the previous sentence. What do we learn from the previous sentence? Quantum computers could *eventually* be used to crack codes that cannot be broken today. What does the sentence in question tell us? That *current* commercial interest in quantum computing is focused on the *much simpler* task of identifying real security threats. Those are two contrasting goals, so a reversal word is required. *However* is the only answer that falls into that category, so C) is correct.

9. A

Nevertheless and *However* have the same meaning, so both B) and C) can be eliminated immediately. *In particular* does not fit either because the information following the transition is not specifying an idea introduced in the previous sentence. D) can thus be eliminated as well. That leaves A), *Subsequently*, which logically indicates that Kennedy gave Roosevelt's executive order to his Marine Commandant after discovering the document himself.

10. B

The two sentences focus on the same main idea, namely that human activities are posing an increasingly serious danger to health and the natural world. A transition that indicates a continuation must therefore be used. *However* and *conversely* indicate a reversal and also have very similar meanings, so both A) and C) can be eliminated. *At any rate* does not imply a continuation either, so D) can be eliminated as well. B) is correct because *moreover* correctly indicates that the second sentence is continuing the idea begun in the first sentence.

Set #2

1. B

The previous sentence indicates that *studies [about the anti-inflammatory power of cherry juice] are inconclusive*, and the sentence begun by the transition provides a specific example of something that is *not clear* from the study (*why cherry juice reduced pain but did not significantly affect range of motion*). Those are similar ideas, so a transition indicating a continuation is required. *Regardless* does not indicate a continuation either, so A) can be eliminated. *Nevertheless* and *even so* indicate a reversal, so C) and D) can be eliminated as well. That leaves B), which correctly indicates that the final sentence is describing a *particular* instance of an inconclusive aspect of the study.

2. D

The second sentence describes a result of the first: if the healthcare sector expands rapidly, then demand for registered nurses will logically increase. The correct transition must convey that cause-and-effect relationship. *Consequently* is the only option consistent with it, making D) correct.

3. A

The previous sentence refers to *one possibility* (building thicker walls), so the sentence begun by the transition must logically describe another possibility (using flying buttresses). The correct transition must convey that contrasting relationship. *Consequently* and *hence* indicate a cause-and-effect relationship and are also synonyms, so B) and C) can be eliminated. *Finally* is used to continue/conclude an idea, so D) can be eliminated as well. *Alternatively* fits because this transitional word conveys the idea that flying buttresses were proposed as an alternative to thicker walls.

4. C

The beginning of the passage tells us that Whyte's focus in *Street Corner Society* was **not** on established institutions, and the sentence begun by the transition supports that idea by listing the established institutions (family, church, schools) that Whyte *barely mentioned*. As a result, a transition indicating continuation is required. *Nonetheless* would indicate a reversal, so A) can be eliminated. *In other words* is incorrect because the sentence in question is not restating or clarifying information from the previous sentence. B) can therefore be eliminated. Even though *similarly* indicates a continuation, D) is incorrect because this transitional word is used to introduce a new piece of information. Here, that is not the case—one sentence builds on and emphasizes the information in the previous sentence. The most appropriate transition to indicate that emphatic relationship is *indeed*, making C) correct.

5. B

This is the rare question that requires you to look only at the sentence in which the transition appears, rather than at the relationship between that sentence and the previous sentence. The sentence in question presents us with two pieces of information: 1) Japanese trade was heavily restricted, and 2) Hokusai's print was influenced by Dutch (that is, foreign) art. Those are contrasting statements, so a reverser is required. *Although* is the only option that fits, making B) correct.

6. A

Logically, the sentence begun by the transition and the previous sentence describe two related occurrences related to the explosion of the meteor (seeing something blue streak across the sky; hearing a crash and feeling the earth tremble). The most logical connection between these events is that one happened before the other: people saw the blue object streak across the sky before they heard a crash. *Subsequently* conveys that relationship, making the A) the answer. *In sharp contrast* and *Yet* do not make sense at all, so C) and D) can be eliminated. Be careful with B), though. While the two events described are part of the same overall series of occurrences, they focus on different aspects of it: seeing an object in the sky is not like hearing a crash. *Similarly* is thus not appropriate here.

7. D

The passage indicates that one in nine Germans read a newspaper in 1850, as compared to one in two 40 years later. That's a very big difference, so a transitional word indicating that contrast is required. *Therefore*, *in fact*, and *furthermore* are all used to continue ideas. Only *however* conveys a contrast, making D) correct.

8. B

The beginning of the passage indicates that the invention of the photographic portrait resulted in predictions that portrait painting would disappear; the sentence in question confirms that the prediction was correct, and that artists stopped creating realistic images. Those are two parts of the same idea, so a continuer is required. *Nevertheless* and *despite this* indicate a reversal, so A) and C) can be eliminated. D), *thus*, does not fit because artists' abandonment of realism was not the result of *predictions* that portrait painting would become obsolete. Rather, it resulted from the invention of the camera. *In fact* correctly emphasizes the accuracy of the prediction mentioned in the previous sentence. B) is thus correct.

9. D

Remember that if you are ever given a no transition/DELETE option, you should always check it first. In this case, that strategy would pay off: there is no transition among the answer choices that would make sense. *Therefore* and *As a result* have the exact same meaning, so both A) and B) can be eliminated. C) is also incorrect because the statement that AI will speed up diagnoses is consistent with the idea that AI will change how medicine works, and *However* indicates a contradiction. The transition should thus be deleted, making D) correct.

10. C

The passage states that plant breeders will use newly discovered information about the genetic makeup of *Coffea arabica* to improve on the coffee plant. The sentence in question provides a specific example of changes that might result (new flavors, better resistance to cold). The transition that best conveys that relationship is C), *for instance*. *However* and *nevertheless* have the same meaning and indicate a contrast, eliminating A) and D). Be careful with B): the last sentence uses specific examples to illustrate the general idea introduced in the previous sentence, but *as a rule* would imply that the last sentence was presenting a general idea. So even though this transition might sound like a plausible answer, it does not actually make sense.

Part III: The Essay

Chapter 5: Key Essay Vocabulary

If you choose to write the SAT Essay, you will be given 50 minutes to read and evaluate a 650-750 word passage from a contemporary non-fiction work. The author or authors will examine a current issue, such as supporting public libraries, providing funding for NASA space projects, or reducing dependence on energy consuming air-conditioners. Your job is to neither agree nor disagree with the author's point of view, but rather to analyze how the author uses persuasive devices to build an argument.

Two readers will score your essay, with each one awarding it between 1 and 4 points in three categories: Reading, Analysis, and Writing. Each reader can give your essay a score ranging from a low of 3 to a high of 12. The combined score of the two readers will thus range from a minimum of 6 to a maximum of 24.

This chapter is not intended to provide you with a detailed template for how to analyze the passage or write a complete essay. Instead, our goal is to focus on two key areas that will significantly boost your score. First, we will summarize seven key points about the Essay task. Second, we will provide you with a unique discussion of how to earn the highest possible score on the Writing component.

Write the Essay

The SAT Essay is optional and does not count toward your 1600 score. You can leave after completing the Reading, Writing, and Math sections. So, should you stay or should you go? Some colleges require the Essay, but many do not. If you are absolutely certain the colleges you are applying to do NOT require an Essay score, your decision is straightforward—GO! Similarly, if you are absolutely certain that the colleges you are applying to DO require an Essay score, your decision is also straightforward—STAY!

The problem is that like most students, you will probably apply to a large number of colleges, some of which will most likely require an Essay score. **It is important to know that you cannot take the Essay separately from the rest of the SAT.** Given these facts, we strongly recommend that you write the Essay.

The College Board Gives You the Thesis

The author's central argument is not a secret. In fact, you do not even need to read the passage to identify it! Begin by immediately going to the box at the end of the passage. The first sentence will clearly state the author's main claim. Here is an example: "Write an essay in which you explain how Jimmy Carter builds an argument to persuade his audience that the Artic National Wildlife Refuge should not be developed for industry."

Identify the Author's Main Persuasive Devices

The College Board chooses passages that employ a number of persuasive devices. The following six devices are the major ways authors build their arguments. While all six may not be present in a given essay, you can count on finding at least four.

1. Providing Facts and Statistics

- Helps the author define the scope of a problem.
- Grounds the author's argument in reality, thus establishing a firm foundation for the main claim.
- Gives the author credibility and makes him or her seem like an authority.

2. Addressing a Counterargument

- Helps establish the author's credibility as someone who recognizes opposing points of view.
- Demonstrates that the author's central claim is well thought-out and not one-sided.

3. Recalling a Personal Anecdote

- Demonstrates the author's personal connection to the issue.
- Enables readers to make a vicarious connection to the author's central claim.

4. Citing Respected Authorities

- Demonstrates that the author's argument is well-researched.
- Builds trust in the author's argument.
- Strengthens the author's credibility by showing that he or she is not the only one who advocates a policy position.

5. Appealing to the Reader's Emotions

- Uses emotionally charged words to evoke strong feelings.
- Develops an emotional connection with or sense of pathos toward the author's position.
- Engages the reader by arousing feelings of alarm, guilt, enthusiasm, or patriotism.
- Arouses a feeling of alarm to alert readers to the seriousness of a problem.

6. Crafting a Logical Argument

- Demonstrates the connection between the evidence and the author's central claim.
- Identifies the major benefits that can be achieved by supporting the author's central claim.
- Demonstrates a cause-and-effect relationship between what is happening now and what could happen in the future.
- Leads the reader to conclude that the benefits of the author's recommendation outweigh the drawbacks of doing nothing.

Select Three Persuasive Devices

As you read the passage circle, underline, or bracket examples of how your author builds his or her argument. Then select the author's **three** best-documented arguments. These persuasive devices will form the body paragraphs of your essay.

Write a Five-Paragraph Essay

Your essay should begin with an introduction that concludes with a clear thesis statement indicating the three persuasive devices you will describe and analyze. You should then devote a full paragraph to each of these three persuasive devices. Each body paragraph should include at least one quotation from the passage and an analysis of how the specific devices used are intended to affect the audience. You should conclude your essay with a short paragraph restating your thesis and key points.

Avoid Taking a Personal Stance

The author of your passage will express a strong central claim. Your job is to analyze how the author builds his or her argument. You job is NOT to inject your personal opinions into your essay. Above all, never use the word *I*.

Write a Fully Developed Essay

Length is an important feature of a high-scoring essay. College Board readers will equate length with a fully developed essay. You should strive to write 2 to 2.5 pages out of the 4 pages provided by the College Board.

How to Earn an 8 for Writing

The College Board's official rubric identifies six characteristics that will enable each reader to award your essay a 4:

1. An overall sense of cohesiveness
2. A precise central claim
3. A skillful introduction and conclusion
4. A highly efficient progression of ideas
5. A wide variety of sentence structures
6. A consistent use of precise word choices

Cohesive, precise, skillful, and highly effective writing requires hard work and practice. It also helps to have models of what these characteristics actually look like. This section is designed to provide you with specific examples of Level 8 SAT Essay Writing. Studying examples taken from real student essays will help you begin your essay with a skillful introduction, develop it with a smooth transitions, end it with an effective conclusion, and enrich it with well-chosen descriptive vocabulary and a variety of sentence structures. Let's do it!

Write a Skillful Introduction

First impressions are important in interviews and in good writing. A skillful introduction will make a positive first impression by grabbing your reader's attention, providing a precise central claim, and demonstrating your command of good writing. Believe it or not, you can accomplish this in just 3-5 sentences.

Use a Hook to Grab Your Reader's Attention

Your opening sentences should provide a hook that grabs the reader's attention by skillfully introducing the passage's overall theme. Here are three examples:

1. Air-conditioning can be a reprieve from the oppressive heat of a long summer day. But it comes at a price. In his article...

2. Art is a window to the human soul. But what happens when this window is shattered? This is the case of the Parthenon, a Greek temple in Athens, whose most famous sculptures are in the British Museum in London. In his essay...

3. "It is a sin to kill a Mockingbird." These eight words are one of the most famous quotes from Harper Lee's classic novel *To Kill A Mockingbird*. The sentiment that the innocent should be protected is shared by the two authors of the article...

These three examples illustrate different but highly effective opening techniques. The first example engages the reader's attention with a general opening statement followed by a short but powerful reversal: *But it comes at a price*. Known as a "punch-line sentence," this short declarative statement alerts readers to an unconventional passage with a surprising argument.

Our second example begins with a general philosophical statement. The author then avoids a dull opening by immediately posing an attention-grabbing rhetorical question: *But what happens when this window is shattered?* The rhetorical question allows the writer to provide an answer that introduces the passage's central claim.

Our third example draws the reader in by quoting from a well-known novel. Like the second example, this option retains the reader's interest by commenting on the quotation and making clear its relevance to the passage's central claim.

State Key Facts About the Passage

Your next sentence is easy. Simply write a straightforward sentence stating the author's name, the title of the essay, and the author's central claim. Here are three examples:

1. In his article "Viewpoint: Air-Conditioning Will Be the End of Us," Eric Klinenberg argues that Americans need to significantly reduce their reliance on air-conditioning.

2. In his article "The Love of Stone," Christopher Hitchens builds an argument to persuade his readers that the original Parthenon sculptures should be returned to Greece.

3. In their article "Bad for the Birds, Bad for All of Us," John W. Fitzpatrick and George Fenwick advocate for the continued funding of wildlife conservation programs.

These succinct sentences provide readers with the required details about the passage. **Remember: the College Board clearly states the author's central claim in the first sentence of the box at the end of the passage.**

Establish a Precise Claim

Your introduction should conclude with a sentence that conveys your thesis by indicating three persuasive devices the author uses to build his or her argument. Here are three examples:

1. The author crafts a persuasive and compelling argument by recalling a memorable personal anecdote, addressing a counterargument, and providing an array of facts and statistics.

2. The author builds a persuasive argument by appealing to the reader's sense of injustice, emphasizing logical artistic benefits, and addressing a prevalent counterargument.

3. The authors build a convincing argument by documenting their claim with facts and statistics, pointing out logical benefits, and making use of a subtle appeal to the readers' emotional affinity for preserving natural habitats.

These three concluding examples do more than just present the author's precise central claim. They also use parallel structure to demonstrate stylistic variation, and employ strong, precise vocabulary such as *compelling*, *prevalent*, *array*, and *affinity*.

The full impact of each example becomes clear when it is combined with other sentences to create a full introductory paragraph. Special thanks to Julia Garaffa and Ben Yao for sharing excerpts from their outstanding essays!

Introduce Each Body Paragraph

The College Board scoring rubric rewards essays that contain "a highly effective progression of ideas." The phrase "progression of ideas" refers to the way you introduce each of your three body paragraphs. This often-overlooked feature is an important characteristic of an advanced essay. Our experience indicates that readers will reward essays that include skillful transitional sentences.

How to Begin Your First Body Paragraph

Now that you have written a skillful introduction, your next task is to provide your College Board readers with a strong sentence introducing your first body paragraph. Here are three examples:

1. Klinenberg begins his argument by recounting a personal experience with the problems caused by excessive use of air-conditioning.

2. Hitchens begins crafting a convincing argument by providing important background information about the damages inflicted upon the Parthenon.

3. Fitzpatrick and Fenwick begin by providing a series of alarming statistics about plummeting bird populations across the Midwest.

All three of these examples utilize a topic sentence that clearly introduces the persuasive argument to be discussed in the first body paragraph. Note that the authors avoid cliché opening lines such as *For their first argument...* or *Let's begin by discussing...*

How to Begin Your Second Body Paragraph

Creating a highly effective transition from your first to your second body paragraph requires an advanced level of writing. Here are three generic examples that you can use in any essay:

1.   The author continues his/her line of argumentation by presenting a series of pertinent facts and statistics.

2.   The author now disarms his/her critics by addressing a widespread counterargument.

3.   The authors further enhance their argument by outlining the benefits of following their recommended policy and the drawbacks of ignoring it.

These three generic examples all use a strong active voice to introduce the author's second persuasive argument. Note the use of precise words such as *pertinent* (relevant), *disarm*, and *enhance*.

How to Begin Your Third Body Paragraph

Transitional sentences are the glue that connects your ideas. Writing an advanced five-paragraph essay requires a toolbox filled with great transitional sentences. Don't worry—we are up to the challenge! Here are three generic examples that will enable you to make a smooth transition to your third and final body paragraph:

1.   The author does more than just cite authorities and appeal to his/her reader's emotions; he/she also uses statistical evidence to document the imperative need for the public to support…

2.   The author does more than just recount a personal story and address a counterclaim; he/she also makes a strong logical case for supporting…

3.   The author is not content to build an argument that relies exclusively on objective facts and logic; he/she concludes by making a direct appeal to the reader's sense of justice.

These three examples all provide the College Board readers with a bridge connecting the previous two body paragraphs with the final body paragraph.

Note that while these examples are not stuffed with ten-dollar words, they do make use of moderately sophisticated terms that give the writing less of a typical "high school" feel. For instance, the first example uses *imperative* rather than *urgent*; the second example uses *recount* rather than *tell*; and the third example uses *exclusively* rather than *only*. In all cases, however, the use of these types of terms is very restrained—it is not intended to show off the writer's vocabulary but rather to indicate that the writer is well acquainted with the conventions of standard academic writing.

Note also that all three examples utilize a variety of complex sentence structures that demonstrate advanced writing ability. Each option begins by referring to a previously discussed persuasive device (e.g. citing authorities and appealing to the reader's emotion) in order to more effectively emphasize that the author employs other forms of persuasion as well. This strategy of "referring back" creates a sense of flow and continuity within the essay—a key component of cohesiveness.

Write a Skillful Conclusion

The College Board rubric for an advanced Level 8 Writing score requires a skillful conclusion. Your conclusion should not contain new information. Instead, it should reinforce your thesis.

Your First Sentence

This sentence should provide a brief restatement of the author's claim. Here are three examples:

1. Klinenberg offers his readers a cogent argument to support measures that reduce our wasteful reliance on air-conditioning.

2. Hitchens voices a compelling argument to persuade his readers that the British Museum should return the original Parthenon sculptures to Greece.

3. Fitzpatrick and Fenwick offer convincing arguments why their readers should support the Conservation Reserve Program.

These three examples all perform the required task of providing a precise summary of the author or author's central claim. Note how the first example slips in an excellent vocabulary word, *cogent*, in a very subtle and appropriate way.

Your Final Sentence

The finish line is now just one sentence away! Now is the time to leave your two College Board readers with a strong concluding sentence that demonstrates your skillful command of writing. Here are three examples:

1. He accomplishes this feat of building a convincing argument by recalling a memorable personal anecdote to establish a connection with his readers, addressing a counterargument to persuade skeptics, and providing key facts and statistics to substantiate his claim.

2. He builds a compelling argument by appealing to his reader's emotions to evoke a sense of outrage, emphasizing artistic benefits to persuade open-minded readers, and addressing a counterargument to demonstrate that he understands all sides of a complex issue.

3. The co-authors make a forceful case by using statistics to document the growing peril faced by wildlife, underscoring key benefits to persuade cost-conscious critics, and appealing to emotions to evoke a feeling of responsibility to preserve natural habitats.

These concluding sentences all summarize the key points developed in the essay's body paragraphs. They do this by using parallel structure to reiterate how each argument affects the readers.

Precise Word Choice

As we've seen, the SAT Essay scoring rubric rewards writing that "demonstrates a consistent use of precise word choice." Precise word choice means using a strong descriptive vocabulary that clearly expresses and defines your thoughts.

College Board readers will not be impressed if you use too many big words, so don't overdo it by being bombastic (overblown). Instead, try to include well-chosen descriptive words that are neither too casual nor too formal. So while you shouldn't start throwing around terms like *reprobate* or *recondite*, you should also avoid words like *things* and *awesome*. (Recall that SAT Writing passages are designed to emphasize this type of writing as well.)

Students often make the mistake of using words they don't fully understand, or that are too extreme for a particular situation. For example, one student described former President Clinton as a "revered" authority. While President Clinton is a knowledgeable leader, he is not considered someone who deserves the type of respect that borders on worship. The incorrect use of words like *revered* is a red flag that will catch your reader's attention and possibly cost you a point. As a general rule, if you aren't 100% of how a word should be used, you should avoid including it altogether.

Keep in mind that passages are written by established authors who present reasoned arguments using restrained language. These articles do not lend themselves to essays using extreme words such as *amazing*, *horrific*, or *atrocious*. Instead, they support the use of moderate words such as *cogent*, *discerning*, and *pivotal*.

You must also be careful to avoid too much repetition. While the Essay assignment requires that you consistently refer back to the author or authors' points, you should make sure to vary the way in which you introduce those points. For example, you do not want to rely excessively on the verbs *say*, *state*, and *tell* (e.g. *At the end of the introduction, the author states… In the second paragraph, the author says…*). Instead, you should also try to include an array of precise verbs such as *conveys*, *illustrates*, *implies*, *(re)affirms*, or *recounts*.

The list that begins on the following page includes 25 carefully chosen descriptive words and pairs of synonyms that students have successfully used in their essays. We define each word and then provide you with a generic sentence that can be adapted to most essays.

Top Essay Words

1. **Alleviate** – to lessen, mitigate, assuage
   The author believes that his/her proposal will begin **alleviating** a serious problem.

2. **Assert(ion)** – claim
   The author supports this **assertion** by using statistics to bolster his/her argument.

3. **Audacious** – showing great boldness
   Aware that timid solutions will not fully address the problem, the author proposes an **audacious** plan of action.

4. **Buttress, Bolster** – to support, strengthen
   The author uses an array of statistical evidence to **buttress/bolster** his/her argument that…

5. **Cogent** – convincing, persuasive, forceful
   The author crafts a **cogent** argument designed to convince his/her readers to support…

6. **Convey** – indicate, make clear
   The author **conveys** a sense of urgency by making a strong appeal to the reader's emotions.

7. **Credibility** – believability, reliability
   The author establishes his/her **credibility** by citing a variety of reputable sources.

8. **Discerning** – demonstrating keen insight
   The author's **discerning** analysis underscores his/her use of logic to address a difficult issue.

9. **Eminent** – well-known, prominent, renowned
   The author cites an **eminent** authority to buttress his/her argument that…

10. **Empathy** – a feeling of great compassion, the ability to put oneself in another person's shoes
    The author's personal anecdote activates the reader's sense of **empathy** towards the human drama expressed by the author.

11. **Enumerate** – provide a list of
    The author **enumerates** the advantages of this possibility by using a variety of persuasive devices.

12. **Evenhanded** – fair to all sides
    The author's **evenhanded** presentation of the counterargument demonstrates his/her lack of extreme bias.

13. **Evoke, Elicit** – produce, call forth
    The alarming lack of financial support for space technology is designed to **evoke/elicit** a sense of urgency among readers.

14. **Idealist(ic)** – a person who presents things as they should be rather than as they are
    The author is not an impractical **idealist**; instead, he/she is a pragmatist committed to offering the public practical solutions to difficult problems.

15. **Imperative** – necessary and urgent
The author concludes by explaining why it is **imperative** that the public support his/her program of action.

16. **Pertinent** – relevant
The author uses **pertinent** data to pinpoint the true dimensions of the problem.

17. **Pivotal** – decisive, critical
The author convincingly demonstrates that we are at a **pivotal** point in our effort to…

18. **Poignant** – touching, heartrending, very sad
The author's **poignant** personal story is intended to elicit a sympathetic response from the reader.

19. **Pragmatic, Prudent** – practical, realistic
The author is a **pragmatic/prudent** leader who is committed to offering a realistic solution to a complex problem.

20. **Ramifications** – the consequences of an action or event
According to the author, the **ramifications** of taking no action will have a number of serious consequences.

21. **Reaffirm** – to make a renewed commitment to do something
The author concludes by calling upon the public to **reaffirm** its commitment to supporting…

22. **Recount** – narrate, tell
The author immediately engages the reader's attention by **recounting** a personal anecdote.

23. **Skeptic(al)** – a doubter, a persistent questioner
The author presents a detailed counterargument designed to persuade even cautious **skeptics**.

24. **Substantiate** – to support with proof or evidence
The author presents detailed statistical evidence to **substantiate** his/her central claim.

25. **Vicarious** – experienced in the imagination through the feelings or actions of another
The author uses a vivid personal story that allows readers to **vicariously** understand why the issue requires strong action.

Putting it All Together: A Sample "24" Essay

College Board readers reward only the finest essays with a 24. However, it can be done. In fact, many students are earning top scores by putting the principles described in this chapter into practice.

One such student is Annie Li, who achieved a perfect 24 Essay. Annie attends Montgomery High School in New Jersey, and she generously granted us permission to publish her essay. Needless to say, we are very proud of Annie! Notice how she weaves in vocabulary words (bold) and transitions (underlined) in a way that seems natural and avoids heavy-handedness.

November 2016 SAT Essay:
"Bad For the Birds, Bad For All of Us"

Living in a society where different organisms coexist, humans have a responsibility, to a certain degree, to protect other species. In their essay "Bad for the birds, bad for all of us," John W. Fitzpatrick and George Fenwick **advocate** for the support of the U.S. government in continuing to fund conservation programs. The two build a **compelling** argument by appealing to emotions, presenting facts and statistics, and using logical reasoning.

Fitzpatrick and Fenwick begin their argument by **invoking** a sense of urgency among the readers. As they introduce the issue of declining bird populations, they <u>further</u> explain that it may lead to "bigger ecosystem disruptions that affect us all" (Paragraph 1). By appealing to the reader's fears that environmental dangers are on the horizon, the authors establish the concern as an **imperative** threat to the well-being of all Americans. <u>Consequently,</u> the audience is more compelled to listen to their argument and to take action; the authors build the trust of their audience, as they are presenting a solution to help them and the society as a whole.

The authors continue their line of argumentation by using facts and statistics to **buttress** their claim. They express the declines of bird populations with facts: "population has plummeted 70 percent since 1970 (paragraph 2). <u>Further,</u> the two authors **assert** that the population of the Henslow's Sparrow "are more than 25 times greater than they were in 1985" (paragraph 3). The increasing population is due to the implementation of the farm bill. By using statistics to express the benefits of the Conservation Reserve Program, Fitzpatrick and Fenwick establish themselves as knowledgeable researchers, rather than impractical **idealists**. <u>Further,</u> the readers are more likely to listen to their **cogent** argument because it is **substantiated** with statistics derived from accurate research.

Fitzpatrick and Fenwick <u>further</u> push for federal support of conservation programs by using logical reasoning. To illustrate that preserving bird habitats also benefits humans, they reason that conservation "yields both healthy food and vibrant ecological systems" (paragraph 8). The authors' reasoning for support of conservation programs extends beyond helping the birds. They appeal to the readers by logically presenting that there are advantages for humans as well. <u>As a result,</u> the audience better understands the reasons for conservation programs and are more **compelled** to support them. <u>Also</u> by using logical reasoning, Fitzpatrick and Fenwick **buttress** their claims, building a sense of trustworthiness between themselves and their readers.

Fitzpatrick and Fenwick successfully voice the necessity of government funding in conservation programs. They accomplish the **feat** of building a convincing argument by appealing to readers' emotions to **invoke** a sense of urgency, presenting facts and statistics to establish their **credibility** as authors, and reasoning in a logical manner to **substantiate** their claims.

Practice Makes Perfect

We strongly recommend that you write several practice essays. Here is a list of eight passages used since the College Board introduced the new Essay format in March 2016. All of the passages can easily be found on the Internet.

1. "Viewpoint: Air-Conditioning Will Be the End of Us," by Eric Klinenberg
    http://ideas.time.com/2013/07/17/viewpoint-air-conditioning-will-be-the-end-of-us/

2. "The Lovely Stones," by Christopher Hitchens
    http://www.vanityfair.com/culture/2009/07/hitchens200907

3. "The North West London Blues," by Zadie Smith
    http://www.nybooks.com/daily/2012/06/02/north-west-london-blues/

4. "Read, Kids, Read," by Frank Bruni
    https://www.nytimes.com/2014/05/13/opinion/bruni-read-kids-read.html?_r=0

5. "Raise the Minimum Wage," by the Los Angeles Editorial Board
    http://www.latimes.com/opinion/editorials/la-ed-minimum-wage-increase-20130913-story.html

6. "It's Time For Paid Family and Medical Leave To Empower Women and Modernize the Workplace," by Senator Kirsten Gillibrand
    http://www.huffingtonpost.com/rep-kirsten-gillibrand/its-time-for-paid-family-and-medical-leave_b_4732451.html

7. "Bad for the Birds, Bad for All of Us," by John W. Fitzpatrick and George Fenwick
    https://www.washingtonpost.com/opinions/bad-for-the-birds-bad-for-all-of-us/2013/08/08/d5a11a34-ff83-11e2-9a3e-916de805f65d_story.html?utm_term=.9cedfb12d252

8. "Space Technology: A Critical Investment for our Nation's Future," by Bobby Braun
    http://thehill.com/opinion/op-ed/190387-space-technology-a-critical-investment-for-our-nations-future

Works Cited

Austen, Jane. *Emma*, 1815. Chapter 3. Accessed through Online Literature: http://www.online-literature.com/austen/emma/3/

Borzykowski, Brian. "Why Open Offices Are Bad For Us." *BBC - Capital*, 11 January 2017, www.bbc.com/capital/story/20170105-open-offices-are-damaging-our-memories

Bronte, Charlotte. *Villette*, 1853. Chapter 1. Accessed through Online Literature: http://www.online-literature.com/brontec/villette/1/

Carson, Rachel. *Silent Spring*. Houghton Mifflin, 1962, spot.colorado.edu/~wehr/309R9.TXT

Cather, Willa. *O Pioneers*, 1913. Chapter 1. Accessed through Online Literature: http://www.online-literature.com/willa-cather/o-pioneers!/1/

Chan, SiNing. "Becoming More Human, One Data Set at a Time." *Medium*, 1 December 2016, medium.com/@evernote/becoming-more-human-one-dataset-at-a-time b3d65d9f2e8b#.6po4i4uo9

Chang, Kenneth. "These Foods Aren't Genetically Modified but They Are 'Edited.'" *New York Times*, 9 January 2017, www.nytimes.com/2017/01/09/science/genetically-edited-foods-crispr.html?_r=0

– – – "Ancient Bits of Rock Help Solve an Asteroid Mystery." *New York Times*, 23 January 2017, mobile.nytimes.com/2017/01/23/science/ancient-bits-of-rock-help-solve-an-asteroid-mystery.html

Copland, Libby. "Feel the Music—Literally—With Some Help From New Synesthesia Research," *Smithsonian*, 5 January 2017, www.smithsonianmag.com/science-nature/feel-the-music-with-help-from-synesthesia-research-180961660/

Cusick, Daniel. "Battery Storage Poised to Expand Rapidly," *Scientific American*, 1 January 2017, www.scientificamerican.com/article/battery-storage-poised-to-expand-rapidly/

Dickens, Charles. *David Copperfield*, 1850. Chapter 1. Accessed through Online Literature: www.online-literature.com/dickens/copperfield/1/

Douglass, Frederick. Claims of Our Common Cause: Address of the Colored Convention Held in Rochester, July 6-8, 1853, rbscp.lib.rochester.edu/4368

Eliot, George. *Middlemarch*, 1872. Chapter 1. Accessed through Online Literature: www.online-literature.com/george_eliot/middlemarch/1/

Finley, Klint. "The Inventors of the Internet Are Trying to Build a Truly Permanent Web," *Wired*, 20 June 2016, //www.wired.com/2016/06/inventors-internet-trying-build-truly-permanent-web/

Gorman, James. "Some Dinosaur Eggs Took Six Months or More to Hatch," *New York Times*, 2 January 2017, https://www.nytimes.com/2017/01/02/science/dinosaur-eggs.html?_r=0

Howard, Brian Clark. "Stunning 360 Pictures Reveal Tops of Giant Sequoias, *National Geographic*, 11 January 2017, news.nationalgeographic.com/2017/01/giant-sequoia-360-videos-drought-water-use/

Krieger, Larry. *The Search for Social Patterns*, New York: Scholastic, 1989.

– – – *The Search For Social Patterns*, 1989. New York: Scholastic, 1980.

– – – Additional works (adapted).

Lahiri, Jhumpa. "A Real Dhurwan," *Interpreter of Maladies*. pp. 70-71, New York: Mariner Books, 1999.

Landers, Jackson, "Escape Artist Harry Houdini Was an Ingenious Inventor, He Just Didn't Want Anybody to Know." *Smithsonian*, 9 January 2017, www.smithsonianmag.com/smithsonian-institution/harry-houdini-ingenious-innovator-didnt-want-anybody-know-180961078/

"These Itsy-Bitsy Herbivores Could Stage a Huge Coral Reef Rescue, *Smithsonian*, 13 January 2017, www.smithsonianmag.com/smithsonian-institution/these-herbivores-stage-huge-recue-coral-reef-180961753/

Langley, Liz. "How the World's Smallest Birds Survive the Winter, *National Geographic*, 7 January 2017, news.nationalgeographic.com/2017/01/hummingbirds-winter-cold-weather/

Lewis, Danny. "Fish Don't Do So Well in Space, *Smithsonian*, 16 January 2017, www.smithsonianmag.com/smart-news/fish-dont-do-so-well-space-180961817/

Limoli, Charles L. "Could Radiation Be a Deal Breaker for Mars Mission?" *Scientific American*, February 2017, www.scientificamerican.com/article/could-radiation-be-a-deal-breaker-for-mars-missions/

Little, Becky. "First Bumblebee Declared Endangered in US," *National Geographic*, 10 January 2017, news.nationalgeographic.com/2017/01/bumblebees-endangered-species-rusty-patched/

Macdougall, Doug. *Frozen Earth: The Once and Future Story of Ice Ages*, University of California Press, 2004.

Nalewicki, Jennifer. "Get Lost in the Landscape that Inspired William Faulkner's Greatest Novels," *Smithsonian*, 9 January 2017, www.smithsonianmag.com/travel/william-faulkners-words-come-alive-rowan-oak-180961528/

NASA. "Dark Energy, Dark Matter," https://science.nasa.gov/astrophysics/focus-areas/what-is-dark-energy

Naylor, Gloria. *Mama Day*. New York: Vintage Books a Division of Random House, 1993.

Panko, Ben. "A Wise Monkey Knows How Little He Knows," *Smithsonian*, 13 January 2017, www.smithsonianmag.com/science-nature/wise-monkey-knows-how-little-he-knows-180961807/

Phillips, Katherine W. "How Diversity Makes Us Smarter," *Scientific American*, 1 October 2014, www.scientificamerican.com/article/how-diversity-makes-us-smarter/

Pound, Cath. "The Serious Artist Behind a Children's Classic," *BBC*, 14 December 2016, www.bbc.com/culture/story/20161214-the-serious-artist-behind-a-childrens-classic

Quammen, David. *Natural Acts: A Sidelong View of Science and Nature*. New York: WW Norton and Company, 2008.

Rieland, Randy. "What If an App Could Tell You When You're Getting Sick, *Smithsonian*, 18 January 2017, www.smithsonianmag.com/innovation/what-if-an-app-could-let-you-know-when-youre-getting-sick-180961847/

Scharping, Nathaniel. "Perception Can Change in a Single Heartbeat." *Discover*, 17 January 2017, 3:08pm, blogs.discovermagazine.com/d-brief/2017/01/17/perception-heartbeat-racial-bias/#.WKHOvldCFCI

Schulz, Colin. "Now Every School Can Access a Fancy Plasma Physics Laboratory," *Smithsonian*, 21 March 2014, www.smithsonianmag.com/smart-news/now-every-school-can-access-fancy-plasma-physics-laboratory-180950234/

Simon, Matt. "A Coffee Renaissance is Brewing, and It's All Thanks to Genetics," *Wired*, 27 January 2017, www.wired.com/2017/01/coffee-renaissance-brewing-thanks-genetics/

Stanton, Elizabeth Cady. Address Delivered at Seneca Falls, July 19, 1848. teachingamericanhistory.org/library/document/address-delivered-at-seneca-falls/

Stinson, Liz. "China's Sinuous 'Lucky Knot' Bridge Has No Beginning and No End," *Wired*, 4 January 2017, 7:00am, www.wired.com/2017/01/chinas-sinuous-lucky-knot-bridge-no-beginning-no-end/

Stone, Daniel. "The Citrus Family Tree," *National Geographic*, February 2017, www.nationalgeographic.com/magazine/2017/02/explore-food-citrus-genetics/

Taub, Eric A. "Would-Be Carmakers Tap the Wisdom, and Dollars, of Crowds," *New York Times*, 29 December 2016, www.nytimes.com/2016/12/29/automobiles/would-be-carmakers-tap-the-wisdom-and-dollars-of-crowds.html

Wanjek, Christopher. "Sleeping Shrinks the Brain…And That's a Good Thing!" *Live Science*, 2 February 2017 02:37pm, www.livescience.com/57740-sleeping-shrinks-brain-synapses.html

Washington, Booker T. *Up From Slavery: An Autobiography*, 1901, docsouth.unc.edu/fpn/washington/washing.html

Zillman, Claire. "IBM Defends the Radical 6-Year High School It Founded To Get Young Minorities Into Tech," *Fortune*, 18 March 2016, fortune.com/2016/03/18/ibm-high-school/

About the Authors

Larry Krieger was born and raised in western North Carolina. He earned his Bachelor of Arts and Master of Arts in Teaching from the University of North Carolina at Chapel Hill, and his Masters of Arts degree in Sociology from Wake Forest University. Larry has taught urban, rural, and suburban high school students in public high schools in North Carolina and New Jersey. His popular AP courses and after school SAT courses helped his students achieve exemplary scores on both tests. For example, Larry led Montgomery High School to a #1 SAT ranking in the state of New Jersey. The College Board has also recognized Larry as one of America's top AP teachers.

Larry's success has extended beyond the classroom. He is the author of widely known prep books for AP US History and SAT Vocabulary and Critical Reading. He conducts AP US History and SAT workshops for students throughout the United States.

A native of Brookline, Massachusetts and a graduate of Wellesley College, **Erica Meltzer** has worked as a tutor, test prep writer, and blogger since 2007. Her series of SAT and ACT guides is currently used by tutors and tutoring companies across the United States and around the world. In addition to *SAT® Vocabulary: A New Approach*, she is the author of *The Ultimate Guide to SAT Grammar*, *The Critical Reader*, *The Complete Guide to ACT English*, *The Complete Guide to ACT Reading*, and *The Complete GMAT Sentence Correction Guide*. You can visit her online at http://www.thecriticalreader.com.

Made in the USA
San Bernardino, CA
19 April 2017